LYCHGATE

LYCHGATE

THE ENTRANCE
TO THE PATH

by

AIR CHIEF MARSHAL
LORD DOWDING

Author of *Many Mansions*

www.whitecrowbooks.com

Lychgate
The Entrance to the Path
By Air Chief Marshal Lord Dowding

First Published September 1945
This Copyright © 2013 by David Whiting. All rights reserved.

Published and printed in the United States of America and the United Kingdom
by White Crow Books; an imprint of White Crow Productions Ltd.

For information, contact White Crow Books
at 3 Merrow Grange, Guildford, GU1 2QW United Kingdom,
or e-mail to info@whitecrowbooks.com.

Cover Designed by Butterflyeffect
Interior design by Velin@Perseus-Design.com

Paperback ISBN 978-1-908733-62-7
eBook   ISBN 978-1-908733-63-4

Non Fiction / Body, Mind & Spirit / Death and Dying

www.whitecrowbooks.com

CONTENTS

TRUTH is hid deep in the heart
LOVE is the magnet which draws it forth
SERVICE is the tool which burnishes it.
Z.

CHAPTER I

INTRODUCTION

My last book, *Many Mansions*, ended with the following words, And so, even as I write the words, I think that this may not really be—*the end*."

It is true that in the first edition the demon compositor left out the last two words, thus completely spoiling my peroration and causing a good deal of puzzlement to my readers.

But it was a fact that that was not the end, and this book is an attempt to relate my experiences subsequent to the completion of *Many Mansions*, just over a year ago. At that time, as I then explained, I had never attended a séance or had any personal experience of the communications or phenomena therein recorded. The book was written from a completely abjective viewpoint. I stood outside the world of spiritualism and examined a cross-section of the existing evidence in the same way as anyone else could do, who had the leisure to locate and read the books with which I dealt.

This approach had obvious advantages, since I did not ask anyone to believe anything except in a judicial spirit, nor to accept as evidence my own personal impressions, which, by their very nature, could not be adequately communicated to another.

A somewhat mixed postbag gives reassuring evidence that I did not altogether fail in my attempt, though a frequent criticism was that there was too much quotation from other books and too little original work. It seems to me, however, that that was implicit in the nature of my undertaking.

Whatever its defects, this book will not be subject to that criticism. Much of the subject matter, it is true, will not have emerged from my own brain, but it will almost all be new, in the sense that it has not been published before. I shall be rummaging, in fact, among the records of a year's personal experience, instead of among the shelves of a library.

This may be a good thing in so far as the reader's interest is concerned, but it will make the book basically different from its predecessor. This book is not written to prove anything on a logical or scientific basis; if dishonesty or undue credulity is alleged against me, the whole thing goes by the board. And yet if my readers will believe that every word is written in the very spirit of sincerity and truth, it may do more to carry conviction to an open mind than did my previous work.

As regards the title, I shall explain later how that came to be adopted. I could not accept a certain suggestion made by my wife, because that gave the impression that I now claimed to possess a wide knowledge of the facts of the future life. This is far from being the case; but the facts, which I do know, I know with that complete certainty of personal conviction which nothing can shake.

Among these are the facts that I am in constant personal communication with my wife and other relations and friends who have gone ahead of me into the next stage of life, and that I have made some new friends whom I have never seen on earth and yet who rank among the dearest and most intimate of my acquaintances.

One rather tiresome aspect of this book will be a tendency to withhold the names of its characters, both incarnate and discarnate.

This is not in accordance with my desire, but the policy is forced upon me by various considerations. People on earth might be willing enough to allow their names to be used, but they are not free agents because of the objections of their relatives.

Again, I have various friends and collaborators on the other side whom I cannot mention by name because it might bring distress to their nearest and dearest who cannot bring themselves to believe in their conscious and active survival.

Lastly the Great Ones cannot allow their names to be used, for an entirely different reason. In *Many Mansions* I gave a relevant quotation from Vale Owen's book on pages 76 and 77. There is a similar explanation from my own dear Guide and Guardian: —

> "You will forgive me my brother if I am but an onlooker on these
> occasions (a visit to a direct voice circle). Although I have had to ask

you to go into the market place and testify, I must remain unknown except to a very small circle. You see I am not yet strong enough to face the great waves of thought, which would be directed towards me if I were known by name.

"I fear nothing from you my brother, because we are one in that, but there are others close to you in work and thought who, in their enthusiasm which lacks all discrimination, might misuse my power.

"You understand that all the power which I command must be used when called upon; hence my reluctance.

"It is not my wish to speak much of myself, but if you can understand that I am but a guardian of certain things, and answerable to my Master for their proper use and distribution, you may realise why I may appear to you extra careful. I am a weak and lowly person, but the power vested in me is great. Lest it be sullied I must walk humbly. "

And so my great and dear brother is and remains 'Z' throughout this book, and, of the continuously active members of our Group, Colonel Gascoigne and my wife Clarice, *obiit* (as the reference books say) 1920, are almost the only ones who can be named.

Other reticences also there must be. This book is essentially personal (though I hope, not egotistical), and I shall give as full an account as I can do of my experiences. But it will be readily understood that these personal experiences may have led me to contacts of which I may not speak, even for the edification of others.

Again, as will be seen from the chapter which deals with Reincarnation, scenes and incidents from former lives of myself and some of my friends have been disclosed. These revelations would constitute some of the most interesting reading matter in the book, if it were permissible to relate them, but that was not the object of the disclosures. They were intended, as I shall explain, to impress upon us the fleeting and transitory nature of our present Personalities, in comparison with the great and enduring Individuality which absorbs and accumulates the lessons of our successive earthly lives, and progresses ever towards ultimate unity and perfection.

The third matter in which reticence is necessary is in connection with those messages of approbation for work done, in accordance with the Great Plan. They are very comforting and sometimes seem quite disproportionate to the sacrifice made or the effort expended. Perhaps some of my readers who are happy enough to be in touch with high levels will know what I mean. I mention this chiefly as an introduction to an amusing anecdote, which I was told the other day. A certain medium upon whom a private circle depended for all its work became discouraged at never getting one of these laudatory messages for herself, although she was frequently used to transmit them to other members of the circle. At length her unspoken wish was gratified, and she received a long personal message from one of the higher members of the Group. The message read, "Without your help we should indeed be handicapped: great is the work which you have done and great will be its results." Altogether extremely appropriate and satisfactory, thought she, until the final sentence, which read, "The Donkey which needs to have a carrot held before its nose is of no use to us."

On reading through *Many Mansions* again I find some things which I should wish to elaborate or modify, but little that I wish to withdraw. Among the many letters I have received are some from earnest Churchmen and women pressing me to withdraw the whole book. I should do no such thing, even if that were possible, because I believe that, on the whole, the book is good and true and fills a definite want in the spiritualist literature of this country. But one clergyman has taken me strongly to task for my statement that "For a hundred years after His death the records depend on a chain of verbal communications starting from His unlettered Apostles, who were patently unable to understand His parables and His teaching, even during the period of His Ministry." He is evidently a deep student of Church history, and he tells me that all four Gospels were finished by about a. d. 90, that it is not the fact that no authoritative form of doctrine existed before the Council of Nicaea, and that the physical resurrection of material particles buried in the grave has never been the teaching of the Church. He concludes by telling me that my knowledge of Church history is on a par with his own knowledge of aviation.

To this last statement I cheerfully assent. As regards early Church history, authorities differ, and I am sorry if I have been to the wrong fountain of inspiration concerning the dates of the completion of the Gospels, and that is all that I am prepared to say.

The variations between the different Gospels suffice? To dissipate any theory that their literal exactitude is guaranteed by Inspiration, and although my correspondent hotly repudiates the idea that their text has ever been deliberately tampered with, this too is a subject on which it will be well to keep an open mind. I shall revert to this in the chapter on Reincarnation.

He, and other correspondents tell me that nobody now teaches that the physical body lies in the grave till Judgment Day and then rises in the reconstituted flesh. But this is a reasonably common belief, as letters from other correspondents indicate, and as the following story will show: —

A lady who is both clairvoyant and clairaudient though not a 'medium' by occupation, was visiting an aerodrome in the Southern Midlands this year. Shortly before her arrival there had been a terrible accident on the aerodrome and the five occupants of a Bomber had been burnt to death. Their funeral had taken place the day before her arrival. She felt impressed to visit the churchyard and did so alone.

When she reached the grave she was mobbed by the five spirits —all in the utmost distress, and wanting to know what they were to do on the Resurrection Day, now that their bodies had been mutilated and destroyed by fire.

She told them that they had finished forever with their bodies of flesh; had they not already got new and perfect bodies? She reassured them and sent them on their way happy and comforted.

But just imagine it! There was not one among those five modern 'educated' men who knew enough to explain the truth to the others.

I must also, in my own defence, draw attention to the fact that in the *Book of Common Prayer*, the Ministration of the Baptism of Infants, and of 'Those of Riper Years,' demands a testimony from the Baptisee or his Sponsors to his belief in the Resurrection of the *flesh*.

With regard to the rest of the book, there is almost nothing that I should wish to withdraw.

I now know that I gave an unduly simplified mechanical account of the Spheres, and my views on Reincarnation are now much further developed than they were when I finished the book.

I did not attribute to Theosophy the importance which is its due in a general search for the truth, and I completely ignored what I may call the constructive and altruistic side of Spiritualism.

All these lapses were due to ignorance, and, if I say that I shall try to correct them in this book, the statement is made in no spirit of confidence in my own knowledge and experience. It is only that the curtain has been drawn aside a little farther, and the additional knowledge which I have gained has but shown me what infinite fields of wisdom still lie ahead to be explored.

CHAPTER II

FROM OBSERVER TO COMMUNICATOR

I must now give some account of the circumstances which have changed me from an objective student and observer of Spiritualism into a regular communicator with the Spirit World and an active participator in the great Plan for the illumination and edification of mankind.

While I was going the weary rounds in search of a publisher (six firms refused the book before my efforts were crowned with success), I continued to receive messages, personal and otherwise, through Mrs. Hill. In May and June 1943 a selection of these messages was published in four issues of the *Sunday Pictorial*, and these articles attracted a great deal of attention, if the size of my postbag is any criterion.

Letters poured in from every quarter, and though it was a physical impossibility for me to answer them all, I have tried to leave none unanswered which came from those in sorrow or from those whose darkness my own limited knowledge might suffice to lighten. It has indeed been a labour, but a labour of love.

I have been repaid over and over again by letters of gratitude from poor bereaved mothers and widows, letters which are like flowers beside my occasionally stony path. Yes, and by grateful messages from the boys themselves, whose own sorrow is lightened in proportion as the black and hopeless grief of their dear ones is dissipated.

I have said that our activities attracted a great deal of attention. This attention was not confined to people living on the Earth. In the spring of 1943 I was swept into cooperation with a great Group of workers on the other side. It came about like this. There is a lady living in Wimbledon who has been clairvoyant and clairaudient since childhood. She is not a professional medium and is in the best sense of the word an amateur. She has little leisure, being a married woman with a house to manage and three children to look after, and that is no light task in wartime. Throughout this book I shall refer to her as L.L. (the initials of the nickname conferred upon her by the Group).

Those of you who have read R. J. Lees' books, *Through the Mists* and *The Life Elysian*, may remember that one of the principal characters was a spirit called Cushna. Well, one day Cushna appeared in L.L's drawing-room, and after a short chat announced "You'll do," and departed.

Very shortly after this I was taken by a friend to call on L.L. when, at an extempore sitting, certain messages were received which convinced us that we were intended to work together.

Cushna visited us and quoted from the last sentence of my book *Twelve Legions of Angels*, written in 1941 and still awaiting official sanction for publication. The sentence reads 'Now, therefore, as I lay down my sword, I take up my pen, and testify.' Nobody present knew of this sentence, or indeed that I had written any book at all.

The association thus began has continued without appreciable interruption to the present date. Cushna is still an occasional if infrequent contributor to our steadily growing records; my own guides took control of the proceedings.

Now you may ask why I, who had never before made contact with the other side, should have accepted these communicators firstly as real beings, and secondly as being worthy of attention and continued attendance; and this is where I find it so difficult to present to you my own deep personal conviction in words which will bring conviction to you also.

If you have read *Many Mansions*, you may remember that in the first chapter I spoke of the five sources from which men may expect to receive information concerning the conditions obtaining after death. The fifth of these was 'Inspired personal communications received through a channel which a man believes to be reliable.' At the end of the chapter I said "There is not much to be said by way of argument about conviction based on personal revelation. If I receive a message from my dead mother which bears convincing evidence of authenticity, not all the argument in the world will shake me . . . I may be right or I may be wrong, but I shall have that personal conviction which transcends all argument."

Well, I have spoken to my father, my mother, my wife and other relations. I have corresponded with Colonel Gascoigne through four separate and distinct sources, three of them unknown to one another. (Colonel Gascoigne it may be remembered is the father of Mrs. Hill, who brought to her the authors of the Battlefield series of messages.) I have never seen him, but I regard him now as one of the closest of my friends.

I have spoken with him by the Direct Voice and have shaken hands with him.

That statement is susceptible of proof by the corroborative evidence of half a dozen witnesses.

As regards my relations with other members of the Group, the evidence is sufficient and convincing to myself; but for reasons already outlined, I shall make no attempt to convince anyone who is not prepared to accept my own convictions. Suffice it to say that I have been associated with Z, my own personal Guide and dear brother since before the dawn of history; and that our personal relations concern ourselves alone.

Another Great One with whom I have close personal relations was a Chinese in his last incarnation, and we know him familiarly as 'Chang' (which incidentally is not his proper name). He is the head of our healing-circle, and is the personal Guide of another member of our Group, who is still in the flesh.

Do not suppose that these are the Heads of our Group. They are among the chief executive officers of the Group, which is itself a section of the Great White Brotherhood. The Heads of the Group are three in number—One I know—One I believe I know —and One remains to be, revealed. I am sorry if you find this incomplete and unsatisfactory, but it is all that I am prepared to say on the subject.

I will, however, give you the words which I received at the end of our first regular sitting. They constitute my working instructions and summarise very well the relations, which still exist between my teachers and myself: —

"Have faith in your innermost convictions, accept the words of no man, let your heart be your guide in truth and sincerity. Seek to understand in humility, offer your service, and in Love shall The Master accept."

At the beginning of the next sitting L.L. said "Here is a frail looking clergyman in a surplice. There are signs of suffering—he is anxious to help—he is one of Z's band to bring messages through."

I thought of all the clergymen I had known but could not connect the description with anyone, then—'Owen Nares—No Owen— VALE OWEN!'

He told me that he had been helping me with my book, and would help me with the flood of letters arising out of the *Sunday Pictorial articles.* He went on: —

"Call on me at any time; I venture to prophesy that you will have need of friendship. You will work against a sea of unbelief. Our friendship and love shall serve as a shield, and the Man of Sorrows shall be your inspiration. Where He leads we can but blindly follow. For though the path is stony and narrow, His handclasp takes away all sense of loneliness. Your work is just beginning, and we are gathering to greet you and assure you of loving friendship and happy cooperation. God bless you my friend; may He keep you in His pathway."

Later Z spoke as follows: —

"When on Earth I was a mighty prince and warrior, and learned responsibility and how to obey. To accept responsibility and to obey are two lessons you have already learned. That is our mutual meeting ground. Your ingenuity will be taxed to the uttermost. I would warn you my brother that you will be tested in the fire to be a worthy member of this band. You must be proved and you must endure. I come not to be kind; I come with a Flail in my hand, and as it descends I shall hold you to my bosom—for such is the Way, I obey commands also."

Then he introduced other members of the Group. I will mention only those who have actively manifested, though all have doubtless contributed their strength and their power to our work.

These active members are Cushna and Chang (already mentioned), Lance (the father of L.L.), R. J. Lees (a Victorian medium and author of Through the Mists and The Life Elysian), James Robertson (a Spiritualist well known in the North) and Proudfoot (an American Indian). One of the most indefatigable of the workers is my dear wife Clarice. This is the way in which we were reunited after 23 years separation.

I had been told that I might ask any questions; and so I asked about my own people, whether they were well and happy. After my mother had come and told me of my father, L.L. said: —

"Here is a lady, very quiet, peaceful and dignified." I said, "Well, that's not my wife anyway; she was always full of laughter and fun and gaiety." Shouts of laughter from Clarice, who always enjoyed dressing up and acting. (She puts on her natural appearance.) Astonishment on the part of L.L. "Why, she has been in my circle for a long time now. I had no idea who she was, or that she had anything to do with you." (To Clarice): "What have you been doing in my circle all this time?" Clarice: "Oh, I just came to see if you were a proper person for Hugh to associate with." I think that this is all that I need say at the moment about our Group. There are others in the flesh who have a common link dating back, perhaps, farther than we know of, and perhaps there may be more yet to be encountered; it is, however, obviously embarrassing to mention individuals by name in such a connection, and there seems to be no necessity to do so.

CHAPTER III

WHAT WE DO

In this Chapter I propose to give an outline of the various types of work which have to be done in the course of our activities.

I say 'have to be done' in spite of the fact that, ostensibly, no task is ever imposed on us. The paramount operation of free will is always emphasised. And yet the task is laid upon our shoulders in a manner which makes it difficult to refuse.

Personally I do not often want to refuse. It is sheer happiness to me when I am able to help the bereaved by passing on news of their loved ones, or by enabling them to regard their apparent loss from a true and wise point of view. I am happy enough writing this book—I don't mind if half my readers think that I ought to have my head examined, provided that the other half can glean something that will help them here and hereafter. I am happy when I am allowed to contribute my quota to celestial activities of which I am but dimly aware. I am happy when I am adding to my stock of knowledge and trying to turn it to wisdom. I am happy to add my own little effort to the work of our healing circle. I am happy, I am supremely happy, when I am allowed to take part in the process of awakening into their new life the lads who have made the ultimate sacrifice for us. But I must candidly confess that the idea of platform speaking was most repellent to me.

An unkind journalist has called me a 'peripatetic evangelist' and I shouldn't mind so much if it wasn't true. The whole thing is so fundamentally opposed to my natural character and inclination.

But, as Cushna has said, "We should all like to choose for ourselves that Cross which we think we could carry with grace and agility."

Of course one gets accustomed to it; 'eels get accustomed to being skinned,' and I must admit that the glimpses which I have had of the results of these meetings more than reconcile me to the other aspects of the ordeal. The physical discomforts of wartime travelling and provincial hotels are a minor but appreciable burden.

Quite possibly the present phase of intensive platform speaking (May 1944) may not be permanent. One cannot foresee the future, and a very good thing too! Have you ever imagined what your answer would be if someone offered to tell you truly, exactly what was going to happen to you on every day of your life, and on what date you were going to die? Would you let him tell you? I know I wouldn't. People consult fortune tellers only on the basic assumption that they are fallible.

I see that I have already nearly completed what I set out to do in this Chapter, but there is one very important activity which I have not mentioned. I refer to the work which we do during sleep.

You may object that this has nothing to do with the work of the circle. Hundreds of thousands of us work in the Astral Sphere during sleep, and probably not one in a thousand has any recollection of his or her activities on regaining waking consciousness. Yet, so far as we are concerned, the work does concern the circle, because we often work together, and always in conjunction with the members of the Group. Also, so far as I am concerned, I should never have any idea of what I have been doing if it were not for the gifts of L.L. When I learned about our sleep activities, I supposed that everybody was so employed; but Clarice corrected me. She said: —

> "You've been talking a lot about people in sleep state. Well, I've been looking into that, and quite a lot of people don't leave their earthly body. They sleep exactly above it. People who actively work over here have been trained. You know you can't do any job without some training."

I shall refer to these sleep activities later on in more detail, but the work done seems to be almost incredibly varied and at least as important as anything that we do in our waking hours. Sometimes it is on the Earth Plane and sometimes in the Astral. It ranges in location from China and the Pacific, through the Burmese Jungle and German prison camps, to the protection of our own Air Force men on Operations, and the reception of little children killed in bomb-raids.

To summarise, then, the contents of this short chapter, the work of our circle consists of: —

(a) The work of enlightening and consoling the bereaved.

(b) The transmission of comparatively infrequent individual messages from identifiable spirits to their kith and kin.

(c) The delivery of Addresses, in different parts of the country, inspired by the Guides.

(d) 'Rescue work.' That is to say the helping of souls in the Astral who do not know that they have left their physical bodies, or who need our help for any other reason.

(e) The work of the Healing Circle.

(f) Work during sleep.

(g) The improvement of our own education.

(h) The conscious contribution of power at the earth-level of vibration, as required by the Great Universal Plan of Evolution.
   (The object and meaning of these activities is not always apparent to us, nor indeed to those who allot to us our tasks. But we accept these duties trustfully as part of the work of our Great Group, and we believe that as time progresses we shall understand more and more.)

(i) Literary work such as that on which I am now engaged.

CHAPTER IV

PHYSICAL, ASTRAL, AND MENTAL

I now come to a difficulty. My general plan is to give you a number of concrete instances of the work which I have outlined in the last chapter, and then go on to discuss, in the light of these new experiences, the problems with which I failed to deal adequately in my former book, to which this is the sequel. But unless I can give you a frame in which you can see the pictures, the stories which I have to relate, graphic and vivid as they are, may seem to be so divorced from what we are pleased to consider the Laws of Nature, as to lay me open to the suspicion of being a victim of hallucination or worse.

And so, before relating the stories, I propose to give you an outline of conditions as I conceive them to exist in the earlier stages of the continuation of our life after death. Just think of this chapter as the picture frame in which I propose to display my tableaux.

Don't be angry with me if I present it in an apparently didactic and dogmatic manner. It represents the conclusions at which I have arrived, and I promise that later on I will produce the evidence on which I have based these conclusions, and that I will not try to evade my reasonable responsibility for saying why I believe such and such a statement to be true.

At one of my Addresses a well-meaning Chairman in his opening remarks gave vent to words more or less to this effect, "Lord Dowding has devoted a great deal of study to the subject, and if a man of his calibre has come to certain conclusions then these conclusions are jolly well good enough for you."

I couldn't help thinking of the nonsense rhyme—

Professor Dewar
Is a better man than you are.
None of you asses
Can liquefy gases.

At any rate it made me feel very uncomfortable. No thinking man or woman should accept the beliefs of another uncritically and without examining, to the best of his ability, the evidence on which such beliefs are based. I don't want a single one of my readers to say "I believe this because Lord Dowding believes it," but I shall be proud and happy if, when you have finished this book, you can say "Lord Dowding has convinced me that, upon the evidence, this state of affairs is more likely to be correct than are other theories and speculations. I will therefore accept his account for the time being, but I will keep an open mind and shall not hesitate to modify or amend my views in the light of better evidence which may or may not come to me in this life, but will most certainly be available to me at some stage in my future life."

And so, I repeat, accept the brief summary which follows with patience, and reserve your judgment upon it until I have had time later on in the book to adduce the data upon which it is based. It will have the further advantage of automatically defining the terms which I shall use throughout the book, because one of the difficulties in the study of Spiritualism and kindred philosophies is the different sense in which different authors use the same terms.

Briefly, then, that little part of the Universe corresponding to the Solar System is divided into seven Spheres, only the lowest three of which concern us at present. They are the Physical, the Astral, and the Mental.

We all know (or think we know) what the Physical Sphere is; it is that which we inhabit in our Earth bodies. Now these bodies are by no means the single structures that the Materialist supposes them to be, nor will the conception 'Body and Soul,' nor even 'Body, Soul and Spirit,' serve to represent the facts. You and I and every human inhabitant of the Earth consist of at least five bodies—perhaps more, but certainly not less. These bodies are: —

(1)   The Physical Body.

(2)   The Etheric Double. This consists of rarefied but nevertheless physical matter which must be discarded at physical death. If it is *not* so discarded, the circumstances may lead to troubles in the early stages of life in the Astral Sphere. Instances of this will be later adduced. The etheric double provides the substance of which ectoplasm is made when it flows from those persons capable of materialising it. Its state of health has an intimate connection with the health of the body, and, finally, it constitutes the substance of which 'ghosts' are built up when something has interfered with the process of its quiet disintegration which should normally take place at physical death.

(3)   The Astral or Emotional Body. This is the lowest, in grade of the non-physical bodies, and is the vehicle of our cruder emotions, such as Anger, Hatred, Physical Love, Gluttony and the like. It is not discarded at Physical Death and accompanies us through our sojourn in the Astral Sphere.

(4)   The Mental or Intellectual Body. This is the vehicle of the lower mind. The reasoning, as opposed to the instinctive mind. The mind that in its higher aspect sifts all Experience of the Mental and lower bodies and extracts their lessons for incorporation in the Individual. In its lower aspect it is responsible for inattention, and wool-gathering, and the idle and futile trains of thought in which we waste so much of our time.

(5)   The Causal Body, or Ego, or Higher Self, which is as high as I propose to go in the present summary. It is itself an emanation from a still higher Spiritual body (or bodies) which remains in higher Spheres and never manifests as part of the complicated structure of which, as you see, we human beings are composed. This Ego (as I shall call it for the sake of brevity) is the final repository of all that is good in human experience, as will shortly be apparent, but I must now break off and indicate the course of man's existence after physical death.

Whenever we fall asleep we leave behind us our Physical bodies and their Etheric Doubles and enter the Astral Sphere. We may range far or near, but in every case we remain attached to our physical bodies by Silver Cords composed of indefinitely extensible astral matter. When, we awake, our higher bodies return to the physical. If we are suddenly aroused, this process is more or less violent —hence the phenomenon of 'waking up with a start.' When we die the silver cords are broken, the higher bodies return no more to the physical, and the latter begin the process of 'returning again to their earth,' as sung in the wild poetry of Ecclesiastes.

Apart, then, from some occasional and temporary trouble in disposing of the Etheric Double, the Astral and higher bodies find themselves free in the Astral Sphere. The important thing to remember is that they feel themselves exactly as they were in the body. The human retina and optic nerve have gone, the human brain is theirs no more, yet they are so accustomed to seeing and hearing and thinking by astral mechanism during sleep that they notice little difference from earth conditions except that colours are brighter and sounds more harmonious. It is true that something seems to have gone wrong with the laws of perspective, but not enough to trouble any but the most observant.

Now the Astral Sphere is divided into seven Planes, each corresponding to a different intensity of Spiritual light, or, in other words, each on a different Spiritual wavelength. The Soul (or vehicle containing the Astral and higher bodies) cannot bear the radiation of a Plane higher than that which corresponds to the wavelength of his own Astral Body (that depending upon his own spirituality, or lack of it, on Earth). By this automatic system souls sort themselves out and go each to 'his own place.' There is no external judgment. But there is this exception, that souls who have earned a greater state of brightness may nevertheless voluntarily remain in a lesser state in order to meet and work with souls belonging to a Plane inferior to their own. (Many of the Air Force men who contact our Circle are in this category, and we may be sure that their self-sacrifice does not go unrewarded.)

It is very dangerous to generalise about the Rules of the Hereafter. Every Cause has its exact Effect and every individual case differs in some respect from every other, so, as soon as one thinks that one has isolated a Rule, an Exception has a habit of appearing to reprove one for presumption, but this Rule, of the capacity for Souls and Spirits to work in. Spheres and Planes lower than their own, seems to be of general application; and it is one of the compensations for the distressed condition of the Earth today that many Great Spirits have left their exalted homes and are working, grateful for even our feeble collaboration, to clean up the frightful conditions which exist on the Earth and on the Lower Planes of the Astral.

The lowest plane of the Astral is Hell—Black, seething, raging, tormented Hell. But here gravitate only those who in Hatred and Cruelty have actively and knowingly and deliberately opposed the Light. Their torments are self-imposed and mutually inflicted, but they are terminable at will. These souls have built up a hard crust around their hearts to oppose the Light; but sooner or later this crust is burned away, it softens and cracks; and as soon as they can bring themselves to cry out for help, there are those at hand whose duty it is to lead them forth and set their feet on the upward path.

The next two Planes correspond with the Roman Catholic Purgatory. Hither gravitate those who have loved nothing but themselves. They live in varying degrees of twilight in a condition of stagnation and extreme boredom rather than in pain. They are the earth-bound Souls, seeking vicarious pleasure from the self-indulgence of those of like mind, still in the flesh, but obtaining small satisfaction nevertheless. Like those in a lower place the crust of their selfishness gradually perishes, and they can be helped by the prayers and love of discarnate and incarnate spirits to rise into the Light.

The three upper Planes of the Astral Sphere are Planes of Light. They correspond to Paradise as distinct from Heaven. They are often called the Summerland. But they have also been called the 'Planes of Illusion,' because here the Soul learns that 'thoughts are things.' Practically any desire that is not actively evil can be gratified by will alone, but the Emotional Body has not yet been discarded and Self is still to the fore. It therefore happens that many Souls tarry here for a long period until they find that these illusory joys bring no permanent satisfaction, and that true happiness can only be found in the immolation of Self and in loving service for others.

Those great souls who have truly learned this lesson on Earth pause but for a short time in the Astral, and, with those who have learned their lesson more slowly, find themselves ready for translation to the Mental Sphere.

This passing is known as the Second Death. It has no grim associations attached to it. It is in fact a promotion which is made the occasion of a beautiful Ceremony, when the Astral Body is finally laid aside and dissolved into the elements from which it was constructed.

The Fourth plane of the Astral Sphere is (naturally) intermediate between Purgatory and Paradise. Its Spiritual brightness may perhaps be taken as equivalent to the average brightness of the Earth.

You may ask, "How long does the passage of the astral take?" I can give some sort of answer in our time; but there is no guarantee that a year of our time has any correspondence in the 'sense of duration' of an astral soul with that which it has on our senses, or that it would have a similar effect on the duration-senses of two different astral souls. Still, for what it is worth, I can give you the quickest and slowest times out of my own 'case-book.' The quickest was the Navigator of a R.A.F. Bomber, who passed the Second Death within a week of the First; and the slowest was an innkeeper on the Dover Road who had murdered five of his guests by smothering them in their sleep. He spent 296 years in the Darkness and so will probably take well over 300 years altogether before he leaves the Astral.

Theosophical books give an average time of about 30 years. I should regard this estimate as being on the low side.

The Mental Sphere also is divided into seven planes—three lower, three higher and one intermediate.

Our knowledge of the Mental Sphere is not nearly so detailed as that of the Astral. This is not unnatural since the higher the development of the soul the greater is its difficulty in communicating, and therefore the number of messages from the Mental Sphere is small in comparison with that of those from the Astral. Also the conditions in the Mental Sphere are more difficult for us to understand.

It will suffice for my purposes, if I say that in the three lower Planes of the Mental, the Mental or Intellectual body is sublimated and finally discarded at the Third Death on entry into the Fourth Plane of the Mental Sphere.

Every good and useful experience of that incarnation is thus brought to the Ego and included in its Aura. Nothing evil or harmful can ever reach the Aura of the Ego. It has either been burned out or paid for by sorrow and suffering on Earth or in the Astral, or else it remains as a Karmic Debt to be paid for at a later stage.

The Mental Sphere is Heaven. The first three planes constitute the Lower Heaven and the upper three the Higher Heaven. The expression "The Seventh Heaven" fits in well with this conception of the future state.

A very important point is that, at the Third Death the 'Personality' of that particular incarnation ceases to exist, and there remains only the 'Individuality,' which consists of the Ego with its Aura containing all the good and none of the evil brought to it by its various bygone Personalities.

In the case of a 'young soul' which has only recently started on the weary wheel of life, the contributions which have reached the Aura of the Ego are inconsiderable. When the Personality evaporates at the Third Death, therefore, the Aura of the Individual is almost a blank. This connotes an existence approaching to insensibility, and the Heaven-time is correspondingly short before the next Incarnation begins.

After each Incarnation the Aura of the Ego becomes more and more fully developed, until at last the happy soul brings to the Ego its final sheaves and returns no more to Earth.

Of course all the above is over-simplified. The Earth is not the only training ground for the Soul. Men may come from other Planets to Earth and go from Earth to other Planets; but beyond knowing that this may happen I have no further information in my present state of knowledge.

Once more let me repeat that, at this stage, I do not ask you to accept the above as anything more than the frame in which I propose to present my picture. It is rather like the Opening Address of the Prosecutor in a Court of Law. In it he outlines the case, which he intends to try to prove.

CHAPTER V

PSYCHOMETRY

I now propose to tell you about the work of our Circle. At the end of Chapter III I gave a summarised list, and I shall deal with our activities in the order in which they were enumerated in that list.

I don't want to deal at any length with my correspondence with the bereaved and perplexed. It was intimate and personal, and not suitable for reproduction. I have only three things to say about it: —Firstly that, though it was a labour, it was a labour of love. Secondly that I was helped by direct and indirect inspiration in my replies. Especially difficult cases I took along to the Circle and was given specific advice. Thirdly I want to thank those kind people who placed their services at the disposal of my correspondents in those cases in which it appeared that a personal message or encounter would be beneficial.

Occasionally (but rarely in comparison with the number of cases dealt with) messages were received in the Circle from identifiable individuals and sent on to their relations. These came not infrequently from men who had been posted as missing, and whose mothers or wives had been wandering round from medium to medium buoying themselves up with false hopes. I do not quite understand why there should be so many false messages in this connection—I certainly don't put it down to any fraud or conscious deception on the part of the medium—my theory is that the intense desire and will of the mother or wife that her boy shall be alive reflects on the medium subconsciously, and results in a soothing answer being given;

e.g. "My Guide says he is not on that side; he has escaped from his pursuers and is being hidden by peasants."

Be that as it may, it has been our sad privilege to clear up many doubts of this nature and to replace agonising uncertainty by a knowledge, which, however shattering, does at least shatter illusions and enable the bereaved to face realities with a strong heart and an absolute conviction in the continued life, happiness and constant presence of her dear one.

These connections are usually made by means of psychometry. Some article habitually worn by the subject is held by the medium. It may be a watch or a wallet or a tie or a piece cut from the lining of some larger garment. It is important that this shall be handled as little as possible in transit. The medium generally begins by describing the personality and human appearance of the subject, and this very often merges into a personal message.

By permission I am going to give you an outstanding instance of this method. Outstanding because of its complete success, outstanding because the mother could be convinced by no other evidence, outstanding because it constitutes a complete proof of survival, and outstanding because the boy in question has since become a very active worker in our group.

The poor mother refused to believe that her boy was dead, although she had the testimony of a wounded officer who was present at the time when he was killed in a tank battle in North Africa.

At my suggestion she sent me an article of his clothing, and here is the result: —

GREEN TIE.

(Hear name of Douglas, Doug.)

This article has been handled by many people and brings confused vibrations. I am breaking through to a youth around 20 years.

Studious and thoughtful, yet light-hearted and ever ready to see a joke. Seems to be humming and whistling. Great love of the country and nature. Music means a tremendous lot to him.

Hesitant in manner, due to shyness he tried hard to conceal. Fine, open countenance, just a boy but with such a fine soul—spirit well developed. Deeply religious in the true sense of the word but has no time for sanctimonious people or anything he feels not genuine. A lover of all beautiful things.

Passing from earth was easy. He was stunned and unconscious of his injuries. Is slowly awakening to realisation. Very eager and alive.

Overjoyed that his vague dreams and thoughts were true in essence. Troubled because of physical parting with those he loves. Very tender and warm-hearted boy. He is conscious of the strong thoughts reaching to him, especially father's prayers.

"As be walks alone in the country he thinks of me. I get the thoughts and thank him for his unselfish love. He bids me 'God speed' and 'God bless' wherever I am. I am very near; a bit bewildered still but this is so wonderful. I have so many friends all anxious to help and explain. Mother, dear (Mumsie, Mumsie) thanks for your prayers and love, thanks all three. Don't grieve for me, I am all right. The music here is something too marvellous to find expression in words. I am not finished, I am only just beginning. Thanks for the flowers by my photograph. You are all three trying to be brave and help me. Help the other boys, too. Pray for us all, we need your prayers. They tell me here I shall be moving on soon. I'm in a sort of half-way house. Things aren't very clear yet. It is clearer as I am touching this woman. You all seem near to me now. Don't weep in your heart. Mother, I'm not lost. I'll be back. I try to play the piano but you can't hear. Leave it open for me."

(He is saying something about a dog. I can't catch what—also an open window looking towards hills.) Refers to a girl—sis—sister who was' thinking of him as she stood on a bridge.

"DON'T WORRY ABOUT ME, I'M FINE. May I come again?"

I want to point out that this is a very complete proof of survival, for those who still need proof. The mother lives in the North of Scotland and had no means of knowing the date or the time when the psychometric reading was being made, and so all the normal explanations of telepathy and thought-transference fall to the ground.

The message was joyfully accepted as accurate in all respects, and Douglas Hoops, and his family still on earth, are enlisted among the spreaders of the Light.

Douglas was a musician and a pianist of very exceptional talent. This bond of music forms a special link with L.L. and Douglas is a frequent visitor. Here is a confirmatory message which he sent a short time after his original appearance on the scene: —

"My name is Douglas. I have been before. Douglas Hoops.

You wrote to my father and mother. Thank you. I don't often go round in the company of Angels and I'm a little bit off my keel.

I want you to know that I have been asked to do this, I would never have butted in on my own.

"Will you be so kind as to tell my mother that I've been again? Thank her, thank them all, for the help they've been giving me. I'm very close and I want to contact, I could through Sis, if they will sit together as you do. I'll do my bit over here, and the Messenger tells me we can get through to them.

"Don (a cousin) and I are to be the Guardians. It's stupendous.

There are several people who want to get in touch. I don't mind dying now that I can see the Plan.

"Will you tell them what to do on your side? They're thinking of coming south sometime; I've been putting the idea through. Please will you ask them to meet the lady (L.L.)? I'm trying so hard to learn my part, and Don too. He sends his love to mother and aunts and uncle and little cousin. We want to start a Lighthouse Sir. Please Sir may I just say God Bless you.

"They're being so brave; but I don't want them (between you and me) to be worrying me to go to these meeting-houses, I don't like the crowds. I like the country and the peace and the quiet.

I was never much good in crowds."

Douglas will reappear later in this book in the Chapter on Rescue Work.

I could give other instances of similar psychometric readings; but they are all rather personal and I do not usually keep copies. In any case I should not publish them without special permission.

I may, however, state that three very successful readings were made from objects sent from Canada.

Before quitting this subject I am compelled to enter a caveat. Will readers of this book please not deluge me with objects for psychometry? Letters I expect; letters I will cope with to the best of my ability; but the work of psychometry is exhausting; and it does not fall on me.

Many mediums have this gift, so please spread the work out among the professionals. I don't say that our Circle will never accept articles for psychometry, but we shall accept them only after permission to send them has been sought and granted after a consideration of the circumstances of each case.

CHAPTER VI

MESSAGES FROM THE PLATFORM

I must now say something about my platform work. You must forgive me if I am a trifle laconic about the circumstances which impelled me to take up a line of work so divorced from my inclination and so foreign to my character.

If you will take my grievance with the necessary pinch of salt, I will say that this is a typical instance of the way in which the Dear Ones cover the Mailed Fist with the Velvet Glove.

They told me that I should be "asked to speak in a large hall." I was so asked and I refused, though I agreed to attend the meeting.

Then I was told that I should again be asked to speak, and I said, "Thanks for the warning. I will let them know that when I say No I mean No." But they said, "Nay brother, speak." Of course they maintain that free will is paramount and nobody is forced into any line of action. All that is true enough I daresay.

But they paint such a picture of the manpower situation in the vineyard—the desperate need of workers and the difficulty of finding them—that one is forced to capitulate.

In fact if the Government would accept discarnate candidates as Ministers of Labour and Fuel, I could suggest those who would have the coal output up again in no time.

But seriously, when one had the following advantages: —

(a) Antecedents which make people want to come and listen;

(b) Workers who shoulder the whole burden of the organisation of the Meetings and

(c) Inspiration and access to completely original illustrations for one's talks; one would be churlish indeed to refuse one's cooperation in the selfless work which is the very life-blood of the Dear Ones: also, I think, one might be very sorry to look back afterwards when it is too late, and see what one might have done but refused to do.

Anyway that accounts for my odyssey as a peripatetic evangelist. Perhaps my work will not continue indefinitely on these lines. Who can say?

Now as to the object of these meetings. They are generally advertised as Propaganda Meetings. I confess that I don't like the word 'Propaganda.' Literally it is quite innocuous, meaning as it does 'things that ought to be propagated.' But circumstances affect words. 'Madhouse' becomes 'Asylum,' but the stigma soon catches up with the new name. And there is something Goebbelish and non-straightforward about the word Propaganda which sticks in my craw (whatever my 'craw' may be).

In any case, whatever the organisers of the meetings may think, my object is not primarily to make converts to Spiritualism. Certainly I want to make newcomers think and to make them realise what facilities exist nowadays to help them in the search for Truth if they want to find it. But my message to them, as also to spiritualists of a certain class, is that the true Spiritualism is not primarily an affair of séances and mediums and phenomena; it is a glad and happy cooperation with the Saints and Angels of God in their loving work of bringing His Kingdom to Earth.

My message is that spiritualists as a whole, and particularly those who are in regular conscious contact with the other side, should reach up ever to higher and higher sources of inspiration. The 'Dear Ones' are always on the lookout for those who are prepared to give willing and selfless service, and to such will soon come the opportunity of making contacts above the Lower Astral Planes if they sincerely aspire to the service of Mankind.

It is, in fact, not too much to hope that the advent of the Kingdom of Heaven upon Earth will be materially accelerated by the activities of little home circles, acting as Beacons in a dark world, and spreading and diffusing the light with which they are themselves irradiated.

I find it rather difficult to write about the third, and actually the most important, object of these meetings. Difficult, because I wish to retain my reputation for sanity and common sense.

Not that I mind particularly what people think of me personally, but because the effect of my work will suffer if I am considered to be a wild and woolly visionary. Visionary, yes, but wild and woolly, no. So bear with me a little, "while I try to explain the unseen work which is done at these meetings, remembering that I myself am only on the threshold of this knowledge, and am dependent on friends on the other side for my information.

Very few Europeans have any conception of the enormous power of Thought as a positive dynamic force. Thought is an etheric emanation which is just as real as light or heat or radio waves, only it is transmitted through non-physical ether, and we need a non-physical receiving apparatus to register it. This apparatus we most of us possess in an undeveloped state, but when we have discarded the physical body we shall see thoughts in their true importance. Thoughts have colour, thoughts have form, and above all thoughts have power.

We can see the results of one man's thoughts in modern Germany. We can see how an orator can stir and unify the thoughts of his audience to religious exaltation, to the heights of patriotism, or to the depths of hatred and blood lust.

And so, even with our undeveloped powers, we can see that thought is real in the sense that thought produces physical effects.

When our limited stock of available time permits, we in our circle are given descriptions of the unseen side of some of these public meetings, and of the way in which the generated power has been used.

I was speaking on this subject at the Caxton Hall in the autumn of 1943, and I think that I cannot do better than to reproduce what I said on that occasion.

A particularly interesting point was that the Caxton Hall had been used a few days previously for a meeting of people whose political views tended to the extreme left. An important political prisoner had just been liberated and these people wished to bring pressure on the Home Secretary to reincarcerate him. They had left behind them in the hall dark emanations which were still strongly present in the hall several days after the event. Of these emanations, more anon.

Here follows what I said at the Caxton Hall.

The Chairman had just read to the meeting the first seven verses of the last Chapter of Ecclesiastes, beginning 'Remember now thy Creator': —

"You have just been listening to some wonderful poetry, mystical poetry, poetry whose meaning is not all clear. But the last words are clear enough. 'The Spirit shall return unto God who gave it.' There is no ambiguity about those words, and they shall serve as an introduction to my talk today.

"By this I don't mean to say that I am going to traverse again all the old ground of adducing* proofs of survival. I am going to do something more interesting than that.

"I am going to tell you how your Spirit, while you are yet on earth, returns to God who gave it, and blends with His Spirit, and helps to do His work.

"I am going to take you behind the scenes at previous meetings and tell you of some of the unseen effects which have been brought about by God and His Ministers with the assistance of the audiences and the speakers, but without our knowledge.

"Now you may think that this is a very fantastic claim, yet it is a sober fact that after most of it he addresses which I am privileged to give you, I receive accounts of what has really been going on.

"Some of these accounts come from seers still in the earth body, and some come from members of the discarnate audiences, which, I can assure you, greatly outnumber those who have secured admission by normal methods.

"It is a curious fact, but the earthly vibrations of people like you and me are necessary to complete the full quota of radiation which is required by God's Agents when they are working on the earth or among those inhabiting the lower planes close to the earth. I am too ignorant to be able to tell you why this should be so, but I know it to be a fact, and a joyful fact, because it permits us to participate in the work of God's Angels while we are yet on earth.

"I am going to start with the meeting held at the Kingsway Hall last September.

"The meeting was indifferently reported in the Psychic papers, owing doubtless to pressure on space. But the outstanding point which I tried

34

to make in my address was the need which the spirits of the dead had for our loving thoughts and prayers. And not only the happy spirits of our own dead, but the unhappy spirits, and the spirits of our enemies.

"Little did I know, as I spoke, how much we earth-dwellers could do and were doing.

"Among the messages which I read out was one from a German boy whose soul had rebelled against the cruelties and crimes which he was ordered to perpetrate, and who had been shot by his comrades in consequence of his revolt. I am going to read it again now for the benefit of those who have not yet heard it.

"I've wanted to for some time and watched but never quite understood how to do it. I am a German ... I know you do not wish to help us in life but in Death we are all the same and the sufferings we have been through have brought us nearer to you and nearer to each other.

" 'I was very young when Hitler took me from my parents and forced me to accept his way of life. It was fine, of course, to be told you are little less than a God and that your lightest wish may be answered if only you follow the Leader. Then came the War and I was sent to Poland, and on to Norway and then to France. At first I was triumphant; then success seemed too easy and it palled; then it began to sicken me and I saw these conquered peoples had what we had not—Love and Unselfishness and the power to endure under our rule—and it sickened me to be sent to kill and bayonet them and harry the old and the sick. My soul was sick with horror and blood and at last I refused to go on and was myself shot by my own comrades. That is all my story but now the worst comes.

" 'I had no one to meet me or to help me. I was alone in the torture and torment that never ceased. A torment of the mind. I could not turn my thoughts to other things as I had done in life. I was obsessed by the crimes and horrors I had committed and those whom I had hurt came to me, showing me their wounds and I was hopeless and helpless and beyond any expression I was damned.

" 'So this is the end to which our vain boastings bring us. I saw it clearly and longed to show others but it was no use; I couldn't speak or move,

I was so weak from the misery; all my strength seemed to go in the agony of enduring this mental torture of my past life.

" 'Then light broke. The child I had been told to kill or wound was killed by another when I refused and she bore witness for me that I had done one good thing; I had refused to kill her, and in doing so I had lost my own life. This came as a tiny light in the darkness through which I struggled, and then some of my own family long since dead, were able to come to me, but they were horrified by the blood through which I had waded and only came near enough to see me; they were shocked that I should have fallen so low, and were not proud of met as a Conqueror or One of the Herrenvolk whom I was always told to revere. I was miserable; there seemed to be no hope; if I climbed towards the Light it only illuminated the loathsomeness of the ME that had survived.

I longed for death to end the long tragedy and give me Peace, but I could only gain that by working in the minds of my old comrades to overcome their brutal tendencies and the task is almost beyond my power. Those who let me write like this, your Father, for instance, are allowing me the opportunity to gather power of this type on the Earth plane, so that I can influence these others who are still with you. I am grateful.

You can never know how much we suffer or how vastly we expiate our sins through suffering of intense bitterness. Franz von Eitelmanrt."

Comment by Colonel Gascoigne:

"Poor fellow, I let him write because we can only influence the Germans through the Germans and that can best be done through their own Dead." Now I will tell you what was really going on; but before I begin I must explain that Mr. Reginald Foort had come 200 miles to play the organ at the meeting and travelled back again the same night. How greatly he contributed to the work will soon be apparent.

This is an account of the meeting by a seer who was present: —

"The hall is full of Air Force boys, Soldiers and Sailors. A little to one side is an isolated group of shadowy shapes. A little above the Boys are Guides and Helpers, and above them the Shining Bright Ones, reaching up and out as far as I can see.

"The Hall is filled with a soft light.

"When Lord Dowding began to speak all turned to listen. Everyone was quiet. A great hush. People in the audience gradually became one with the larger Audience. One continuous Spiral of people, right up into the Light.

"Then a soft rosy glow began to filter through, and as Lord Dowding read out the German boy's story, the lad came and stood beside him.

He was very anxious. He kept looking round at the people, and as he began to realise that there was no Hatred, he straightened up. When Lord Dowding finished reading his story and the clapping began, he looked round with a face so illumined it was a joy to see, and sprang up with one leap to join the Air Force boys, who welcomed him with open arms. At the same moment the rosy light flooded the whole place, strong and bright.

"The isolated group of dim figures was lit up and it was seen that they too were Germans. They moved forward a little way towards the others.

"As Lord Dowding spoke of St. George, the beautiful Cross of Light appeared; and right in its centre was the group of Germans. Then they began to move forward one at a time to mingle with the others and became part of the great host.

"During the music it was very beautiful. The musical vibrations went out in colours, in geometrical designs—each a different colour and shape. As they rose upwards they expanded in size but kept their shape. All intermingled in the most fascinating designs.

"Groups of children picked up the coloured shapes and passed them on from one to another through the whole vast assembly. Everyone was moving in rhythm with the colours: wonderful to watch.

"The culmination came when everyone began to sing 'Land of Hope and Glory' The human voices added little sparks of different shapes and colours to those there already. They were sharper and more brittle looking. The whole thing swelled in volume and everybody moved in rhythm until they were all part of the great cross, so that it was vibrating with every colour, the deep Rose Glow in its centre. It was indescribably beautiful. As the last chord of music struck, the Star of Light shone out at an immense distance and the light streamed from it like a shower of glittering rain and obliterated everything. We were all in it then."

That is the account given by a seer still in the flesh. Here is Colonel Gascoigne on the subject; his account was given quite independently to Mrs. Hill who was not within 100 miles of the meeting.

"Now Sir Hugh wants to know about the great meeting and how it looked from this side.

"We were able to assist with the music; it was a great help. There was a party of spirits turning the mind of the musician towards the atmosphere that he could create for us; and he responded superbly.

Music was the foundation of our success. In other words he built the spiritual meeting-hall. The mighty chords raised pillars of amazing beauty, and the recurring symphonies formed the arches and wove into being a great Cathedral of colour, sound and spirit form.

"Through the help of this medium our power was greatly increased, and we were able to assemble the men who were to form a bridge-head by which the Germans could return to life, and by their help the physical ether was prepared.

"That was our first experiment and it went further than you can conceive. The German chosen for the task was quite a nice fellow until Nazism got hold of him; he was easy to influence and too weak to stand against it; but his real Self was always at war with his conscious Self Now the light is growing round him and he is gaining in understanding.

He brought some friends, but we did not admit all to our Circle: they have to cleanse their minds of all cruelty and selfishness and the desire for possession. That is not easy, nor is it easy for us to close the gates once they have opened. But the Guardian of Light was at the door and his strength exceeded all others; and in the Ray of St. George the voice of England brought merciful forgiveness to suffering ones who had reached the limits of endurance. Light was able to reach their souls and overthrow the evil of the black forces.

"While Sir Hugh was speaking power flowed from the Great Spirit of Mercy who was standing beside him, and many great ones were there too. The St. George's Ray enfolded the whole company.

"Yes, I think I have covered all the ground—the beauty of the music, the Cathedral of colour, sound and form and the Chalice of Sacrifice—that I have not mentioned—the Chalice of Sacrifice is always present when our workers unite for any special duty: it is held like the Holy Grail suspended in the air above the participants, and the rays which emanate from it suffuse the whole building. Beauty, Love and Sacrifice draw the corresponding vibrations from those in the flesh body, and the union of both sides was incorporated in one most blest Communion Soon afterwards a second letter came through from the same German boy. Here it is: —

September 18th, 1943.

"I am deeply humbled by this great experience of death, and then to be re-awakened into life by the nation against whom I have fought, the most bitter enemy to my country. I am deeply touched that you should wish, even a little, to help one who has fallen so low. But I have learnt many things since I came here. One is the lesson of endurance.

We have no power of endurance as your nation has it, and those souls who have gained it are like white lights in the land of shadows. You see I am not yet on the plane of beauty and happiness, because that lies beyond my state of development. But I am learning all the time and I can see the figures clothed in the white light of endurance, and when they come near to me I feel as though God Himself were close, and the end of suffering in sight.

"I have taken your strength to my friends, and brought them into (under) the influence of your great Leader...........

I see it all now, and our mistakes and broken promises, and the results they entail. Thank you, I see the way now. I am upon firm ground.

You have given me back Hope and Companionship. I live again.

"F.Von E."

Colonel Gascoigne:

"We are very sorry for them all; they have no fountain of power to draw from. They have no national church, or body of people whose minds are lifted above the earth plane. That lifting, even for a moment, releases the earthbound stress and gives to that person just so much of the great Vital force. In Germany and Russia they have looked upon death as extinction, and therefore it very nearly becomes true, and there is no national thought store to draw from." And finally this from a much more elevated Source: —

"We wish to thank you and those also who used their earth power to liberate from darkness the Lord's people who had misused His Love.

"Speak also to the Music Maker of our gratitude to him. Without music our task would have been more difficult.

"My brother, the work done was the work of raising into Light thousands eagerly seeking the needed love of Mankind and of the Most High; raising them from beyond darkness to the realms of light.

"Souls were liberated to seek enlightenment, not only your comrades in the flesh, but in other Spheres also." Perhaps on some future occasion I shall have time to give an account of similar messages which tell of the results of other meetings: but I have already told you enough to show you how much you can do to further the loving work of the Great Ones on earth and on the adjoining Spheres—you who have gathered here from so many and various motives.

In parenthesis, I must give you a brief extract from an account of another and later meeting: —

"It was interesting to watch how the barriers of the intellect were gradually broken down by the truly loving thoughts hidden deep in the hearts of the people. Some there were who were a little ashamed to be found in such a gathering. Some there were who reasoned coldly within themselves. Some there were who came only to look at a curious piece of humanity. That was you, my brother.

"Here and there, as always, were the Little Lights: few there were to begin with, but as you spoke they flamed higher and ignited the shrinking lights of others, until at the end, as you will remember, one brave Light forced the others consciously to turn to us. Then did the Power flow, and the heavens rang with joy; for God's creatures were swept up closer to Him and His Power reached to the nethermost pit in a great flash of light. Oh, my brother, could you have seen, or that I had the gift of words to lay before you, the great and glorious picture, when the Master stands, a shining vehicle for His Power, and we may look upon that smiling Face and give thanks for His Blessing. The Radiance of His Countenance when His earth children turn towards Him sets the Music of the Spheres ringing, and all the universe sings for joy."

This platform-speaking is not the kind of work which I should have chosen for myself Those who know me well will agree that I have my full share of the Englishman's inherent reserve and dislike of any display of the emotions. If I must come to the public notice, I would much rather sit in my study and write: but, as one of my great new Friends has said, ' We should each like to choose that Cross which we think we could carry with grace and agility I know now why I am bidden to do this, and I think that perhaps you will realise it also.

The words which I give you are true and important, but that is the lesser part. What is needed for the Work is the Power of the earth vibrations—the Power which you and I can contribute to complete the octaves of wavelengths which are needed by the Great Ones when they are about the Master's business. Give of that Power ungrudgingly and without stint.

How the Power is being used, it is not for me to say. Perhaps to help and guide the counsels of the Allied Presidents and Statesmen but now met in International Conference—perhaps to comfort and solace those in the flesh, who are suffering grief and pain beyond the limit of human endurance—or perhaps to rescue and fortify those unhappy spirits who are so sadly excluded from the prayers of our national Church.

But of two things we may be certain: The first is that the power of collective thought and unselfish prayer is tremendous beyond our human conception, and the second is that no atom of the generated power is ever wasted.

I concluded my address by giving the message from Z, which will be found in the last chapter of this book.

Two days later I heard something of what had been going on in the Caxton Hall while I was speaking.

Relating what she herself saw, L.L. said: "There was at first a black cloud at the back of the hall which advanced up the centre aisle and was with an effort pushed back. When we relaxed, it advanced again.

"The walls of the hall disappeared. There were a lot of little groups of people in 'huddles' facing inward. As Lord Dowding spoke, others came forward, but the groups 'stayed put.' They were arranged round the hall like a U magnet.

"The R.A.F. boys were in a different dimension. When Lord Dowding spoke of the German, they cheered.

"There were the usual groups of Helpers with newly-arrived spirits waiting to be woken up. As Lord Dowding went on speaking, the Cross of Light appeared, slightly above our heads.

"Gradually the weaker shapes were taken into the Cross, bathing in its light. The Cross eventually consisted entirely of newly awakened shapes: the Helpers were concentrating their power inwards towards the Cross.

"At the end, the rays from the Star of Light grew so strong, they filled the whole place.

"Then the 'huddles' were lit up, as if each person were an electric lamp, sending light up and up to other groups above them. There was a feeling that in each group the dark forces were being dispersed."

Chang: "You are perfectly right; the groups were clearing the conditions. You will remember the labour of the dark hours in which you were engaged a little time ago—the transmuting of the hate and passion-vibrations to the vibrations of love. Our groups had been established in that meeting-chamber for a short space before you arrived. The dark flood was not directed against you people; it was the residue of unrestricted passion—of mass-emotion of the worst type. This particular work of cleansing the conditions is one for which I have prepared myself. (Speaking to me) So it was that in the astral world I came very close to you to protect you, as you were wide open to all the winds of heaven. There were some elements there that could have harmed not only you but those others with you."

Z.: "Greetings my brother. You are anxious to know about the meeting and what occurred with us.

"The groups were transmuting those slow, heavy, turgid vibrations. We had a unique opportunity to draw within those groups much of the hatred which is abroad in your world. Each of those shining groups which you saw had attached itself to a group in your audience, and from each member of the physical group was thought directed to a certain part of your globe where hatred wars with love. So, each physical person provided the motive power which enabled the group to draw these heavy vibrations upward and, as they rose, as your words turned the thoughts of all those who listened to you in towards their own hearts and thence outwards towards Him whom we serve, we were able to pass those heavy vibrations to Him.

"He cleansed them and returned them with His Blessing. So from your meeting went out a great cleansing power, which may have this very material effect—that many who are fighting with physical weapons will find their enemy most surprisingly vanquished.

"That is only one effect. That is the effect your own people have sent forth: for the physical plane is most powerfully regenerated from the physical plane.

"On the Astral plane, as those great waves returned in blessing, many who were held by the shackles of sorrow, of ignorance, of desire, found their shackles drop from them, and they were free to move out of the greyness into the Light.

"In the other planes the effect was correspondingly powerful, but to transmit to you in words the work we do here would be impossible. You could not understand.

"I can tell you that, for a moment while you were addressing the assembly, The Master Himself inclined His face towards you because the hearts of the people were with one accord turned towards Him. In that moment His blessing fell, rich and free, on every one assembled there. Many were conscious of that moment and recognised it. To others it was but a momentary flash of great peace—a momentary understanding of something normally beyond their ken. But to every Monad represented there, there was given an added status, a fuller realisation of the mighty purpose of the Creation, a spur to further endeavour, through the personality, to fulfil its mission.

"I have given you much tonight of the inner side of my real work, which is to endeavour so to make Him felt among men, that for very necessity love must replace hatred, and the brotherhood of all peoples become a living reality—for come it shall sooner or later."

Perhaps this sample of what is said at our meetings, and of the unseen events which are simultaneously occurring, will suffice for my purpose of showing how the great Plan is unfolding. I am sometimes a little sad that my own eyes are holden; I would give much to see these lovely and soul-stirring sights. But perhaps things are just as well as they are. My business is to tell the people the things which are given to me to say, and I fear that my attention would be sadly distracted if I were able to see the wonderful events which are in progress while I am speaking. I should be like one of those excitable B.B.C. commentators who gets so excited himself during a football match that he quite forgets to tell anyone else what is happening.

So now I will leave the subject of our Meetings and pass on to the next chapter.

CHAPTER VII

RESCUE WORK

Now I come to what you may consider to be the most interesting chapter in this book; it is certainly the most full of vivid and human incident. It deals with what is commonly known as Rescue Work.

I don't like the term very much myself, because it conveys the implication that those whom we are permitted to help are being rescued from the consequences of their own misdeeds, or that we are engaged in a type of Astral Slumming.

In only one instance of those which I shall quote would this be at all true. With this single exception all the men and women who have been brought to us for help are ordinary decent folk whose predicament is due simply to their complete and absolute lack of knowledge of what to expect on the other side of death. If any are to blame, it is their spiritual pastors and masters, and the lay philosophers of the West upon whom the blame must fall.

These poor lads whose physical lives are suddenly blotted out in the heat of action, pass into the Astral, sometimes without even a moment of unconsciousness. They feel exactly as they did a moment before, they have (apparently) the same bodies and the same clothing; can you wonder if they fail to realise what has happened to them? They can generally still see and hear people who are yet in the flesh, though they cannot make themselves seen and heard, On the other hand their vibrations are still on the Earth wavelength and they are consequently unable to see or hear the

Helpers or Messengers or their relations or comrades who have come to meet them.

Often their sensations are those of men wandering in a grey mist, aimlessly waiting for the fog to clear.

It frequently happens that one or more of these people are brought to our Circle to be awakened. Sometimes they cannot even see us at first, and sometimes they see us from the beginning.

L.L. can always see them, and I can never see or hear them. It was strange at first, but I have now got quite accustomed to carrying on long and intimate conversations with invisible and inaudible presences, depending on L.L. to tell me who they are and what they are saying and doing.

All the time we are talking to them the Guides and Helpers are pouring radiations upon them and raising their 'wave-length' to the astral level. Realisation comes to them sometimes by means of a mild shock—often the result of an attempt to smack me on the back, when they encounter no resistance.

On other occasions we begin to appear to them shiny and shimmering. This is generally a sign that the work has been done and that if they will turn round they will see and recognise some old comrade who has crossed the border a little ahead of them.

More rarely L.L. goes into trance and her body is temporarily occupied by the person whom we are trying to help. Neither of us likes this method, L.L. for obvious reasons, and I because I have no one to tell me who is present and what is happening. I do not know the rules which determine the method to be used, except that, broadly speaking, the trance method seems to be reserved for the more difficult cases.

All our work is done in perfectly normal conditions such as obtain in a comfortably furnished suburban drawing room with no restrictions as regards lighting. Sometimes there are only two of us present, but, when visitors are brought to us after our Healing Circle, one or two others in the flesh are present also.

As you may imagine, some ingenuity is required on occasions to carry on a matter-of-fact conversation and at the same time to devise little expedients to bring home to our visitors the true situation.

The first case in which I personally participated was made very easy for me, I had only to sit and be looked at. This is how it went: Z. "... And now for the work which we have brought for you to do.

"I am glad that my brother has a face which has often been pictured, because he is going to show it to this boy. I have always though); your newspapers trivial and uninspired, but now they are going to be useful." A collapsed Air Force boy is brought in on my left. Denis (in khaki) is holding him on one side and Teddy (in R.A.F. blue) on the other. Z. says he crashed into the sea. I am asked to sit showing my profile for him to see as I write.

Z. and two other Guides stand behind the boy, the four forming a diamond.

The three send out rays, and, as they strike the boy, he begins to straighten up. A great circle of 200 or more stand round and pour power onto the three, who direct it onto the boy.

Boy. "What am I doing here? I ought to be getting back." He can see the room and L.L. and me, but nothing else as yet. "I didn't do anything, sir. It just got me." He is suddenly perturbed by seeing Denis. Denis says: "Sir Hugh can't see you." The boy asks if L.L. is my secretary. I laugh and say: "No, I am hers." He says he went down in the Channel.

Now he sees Teddy as well as Denis and notices the difference in make-up between the 'living' and the 'dead.' He says he was in a Fighter escorting a big squadron of bombers.

"I saw a Heinkel and turned off to engage, and I got the blighter.

These fellows are telling me that he got me too." He is straightening. He is standing alone now. "Well, if you two are dead and I am dead, what about these people?" (L.L. and self.) He has taken it. He knows who I am. He sees us as misty.

"Well, if this is death, I can take it. But I just don't know what hit me. I got the blighter, and I don't remember anything afterwards."

A Voice rings out "About turn." He turns and sees Z. Oh! If you could see his face! He is being taken off to a Home of Rest.

Clarice tells us that two other boys were helped at the same time. "The habit of obedience is strong. The mere fact that they got the order About Turn in your presence helped. They saw us with their minds full of obedience and so they were able to take and hold the great flash which came from Z. Bless you both and thank you for giving us the opportunity to work with you." I can see that my difficulty is going to be to decide what to leave out. I could fill a book, let alone a chapter, with these stories.

But the next one shall be the awakening of two airmen and a soldier killed in the North African desert. I think you will agree that it would make a good curtain raiser for a psychic play.

3/8/43.

Here are three boys, two in Air Force uniform and one in khaki. They see neither the Helpers nor us. They are sitting on a bank. They have created around them the condition of the country in which they died—sand—desert. The two Air Force men are sitting on a scrubby hummock. The Soldier (in a Highland bonnet) is lying on his elbow. He has a smashed knee roughly bandaged. They are smoking cigarettes and talking quietly.

We are going to be allowed to watch their awakening: it will be useful to us later on. They will see us before they can see the Helpers.

The elder (E.) is about 26, he has a little moustache; the younger (Y.) is about 20, he has been hit in the right shoulder and chest.

E. seems to have damaged his leg in some way, though he has not been hit. They are awake, but they don't know that they are dead.

They have created their own surroundings. There are crowds waiting to help them, but the three can't see them. They are talking: —

Y. "Have you noticed anything funny about these cigarettes?" Soldier (S.). "Yes I have rather, but I didn't just know what.

What have you noticed?"

Y. "They take a damned long time to burn. I have been smoking this one for ages."

E. "It's all your nerves. We have got a bit out of focus. It is all so quiet."

Y. "Yes. I've noticed that. There's no sound of firing."

S. (looking round). "Funny. Mighty clean, this desert. It's strange of them to have cleared the battlefield and picked up the wounded, but to have missed us. I don't see any others, do you?"

E. is puzzled and worried. He has been thinking for quite a little while.

S. (Looks at his wounded leg, and moves it in a puzzled way. The other two are watching him intently). "Did you ever see a leg, smashed like mine, that you could move about?" (Sitting up) "Funny, for a minute I thought those bandages were clean." (Drops back.)

E. Is now very worried. He has leaned over and pinched Y.

"Do you feel that?"

Y. "Yes."

E. "Then we can't be." (They start pinching one another.)

Y. "It's queer this quietness and emptiness. I don't remember any place like this. Where is our machine? Of course, we baled out. We probably drifted quite a long way from it."

E. (Begins to see). He has seen me (H.D.). "Do you see what I see?"

S. "I think we are in a room. How did we get here?"

Y. "I seem to know that mug. Do you?" (They can see our surroundings—a plainly furnished top floor room, with a sloping roof, in a suburban house.)

E. "I know who it is! Thank God we will find out where we are." He comes forward dragging his foot. He sees my face, but can't see that I am writing;' nor can he see L.L. Now he has got the whole picture. He is puzzled because I am not in uniform. He wonders if he has got the right idea.

"Excuse me Sir; can you help us. We've baled out, and lost our bearings. A moment ago we were in the desert, and now we 're in a room."

Self. "Yes. You've come home."

E. "Home! That means England."

Self. "This is England."

Y. (Disgustedly). "He's crackers too!"

E. (Touches me and his hand goes through my shoulder). "Do you see what I see, or am I dreaming?"

S. "There's a dame here! I can't understand it."

Y. Looks keenly at both of us. Then he looks round. He speaks to E. whom he calls Turkey. "I have a hunch we've taken the long jump, old chap. I read somewhere that you don't know when you've left Earth. Give the old chap a good one on the back, and see what happens."

Self. "Yes, go on. A good hard one!" E. Does so, and his hand goes right through me. "Is that what you meant, Sir, by Home?"

Self. "Yes."

E. "Well, we can take it. What do we do now?"

Self. "Remember I can't see or hear you; but there are dozens round you trying to help. Try to see them, and you will see us looking less and less solid and natural."

Y. Looks round and sees something. "HERE, they're coming for us!" (Helpers are seen with stretchers. They won't really need stretchers but it establishes their purpose.) Poor S. is very puzzled.

Y. "I read that you don't have any illness. Think that you're well and you are well. I'm going to stand up." (Does so.) "Come on Jock, get up!" S. (Stands up and takes off his bandages. His knee is perfectly healed). "Right. I'm going back to where I started. They'll be saying I'm a deserter!" E. Is rather sad. He has accepted and understood in a flash.

"It's the kiddies I'll miss." He salutes me. "As I've been once, may I come again?"

Self. "Yes. As often as you like, if we are allowed to."

E. "I want to have something to hold on to, someone that I know. They-won't think that we've run out on the job?" (I reassure him.) "I'd better go with the others." Self. "Yes. You will be able to help them. You understand more than they do."

E. (Sees crowd of R.A.F. boys). "Such a lot! There must be nearly as many over here as are still on Earth. Well! If this is the packet we're all facing, it isn't so bad—it isn't so bad—Why, PAT, you old son of a gun! (Recognises friend.) S. Is asleep. They have "given him something." He was less prepared than the other two for the new conditions.

Y. Is excited, and not going to miss anything. He is thrilled because his arm is sound again. "I was an artist. It would have been tragic if I had lost my arm. So long as I have my hands I don't care for the rest." Goes off happily.

Explanation. That is a very good work. To bring them to realisation through Earth makes it so much easier for them and for us. Especially in cases like these boys who gave their all for an Ideal, and are what you would call Decent Lads. Their quietness in accepting helps us much more than you can realise—you who don't understand vibrations and rays as we do. Self Control is helped by the fact of a Superior Officer being present.

(I said I loved this kind of work and would gladly do more if opportunity offered.) Denis. "The boys are all right. We get them lined up for you, and then there is always a fresh lot. (I said how little we could do.) You do a lot in the sleep state, too. If people only knew what you did then, they would indeed say you were 'crackers.' (I asked about Peter.) "We will bring him along some time.

He has thrown himself heart and soul into the work of protecting pilots. His attitude is that there are plenty to deal with those who come over. He is working night and day to protect those still on the job. We will bring him. We will have an interesting Chapter for that Book they talk about." All singing, "For he's a jolly good fellow."

11/8/43.

L.L. "I get the sensation of water. I wonder what that means . . . There is a young Sailor. Very excited. They are calming him down. He is terribly anxious to get back to earth and say that he is not dead. They promised him that he might speak; but he is too excited. His voice swells and fades like bad wireless reception; it is unintelligible—That's better!"

"My name's Cox. I was a gunner, and oh she was a beauty (patting a gun). Can I say how many planes she brought down?" His gun got 15 Jerries. He won't give the name of his ship. (It looks like a destroyer.) "They won't find no body for me, because we got it fair and square. The Padre here tells me I was blown up. I didn't know about that. All I know is that one minute we were blasting away and all Hell was let loose, a noisy Hell, and then it seemed that the next minute I was in the most beautiful and peaceful garden. Just think of it! One-minute reek, and smoke, and noise indescribable, and the next, clear sunshine, green grass, and the birds singing.

"I was a bit surprised like, and thought I was dreaming: then I saw the pond with some ducks on it. I've always liked ducks, cute little beggars, and I thought I'd go and have a dekko. The Padre was there; he was the rummiest Padre I've ever met. He was talking to those ducks, and blimey if they didn't quack back at him! We got talking like; and soon we seemed to be old pals together, both of us liking ducks you see.

"Suddenly I found myself asking the Padre where we were. The place was familiar, yet not familiar. His answer fair blew me down the hatch, because he said 'You are in your own home, one you built for yourself while you were still living on the Earth.' That took some swallowing! But he explained it so naturally, reminding me of the battle. Then he brought me here (Wimbledon) and I watched three airmen becoming aware of their new life. (The Padre is giving me these words because I'm not very well educated.)

"I saw these men were on what looked like a little platform, just like a scene on a stage. It was a desert scene. At first I thought they were play-acting, but the Padre told me to watch closely. These men thought it was real. The Padre told me I could help them because I was more awake than they, *so I thought about their cigarettes, and told them that they had lasted a long time.* It was amazing to see how quickly they caught my thought. That set the ball rolling. Then I saw that there were hundreds of Air Force boys looking on, and sending out a great Light— it looked like a light to me. The Padre said, 'It is a ray of power, and it gives to everyone who can see it, new strength.' I felt better for seeing it. You know what happened to those boys; and, as they saw you, and then saw us, I know for good that this me, though still the same me, is still not the 'me' that was William Cox.

"Then I wanted to know about my mates. Two of them are still asleep in a lovely hospital called a Home of Rest; the other two are waking up like me. We've seen a lot, and I'd like you to tell folks that this is a marvellous place. Don't grieve, don't be sorry for us; we are the lucky ones.

"I am working now with a group of people who help the Sailors over, but I wanted to let somebody know that I'm O.K.—that we're all O.K., and the old saying that God is Good really means something over here. Now I've got that off my chest I can get on with things, and maybe the Padre will bring me back sometime to tell you about what I find here."

You will have noticed the connection between these two stories.

The Padre, incidentally, was Vale Owen.

The next episode is the awakening of a Bomber crew, shot down over the Ruhr. James brings the pilot to us. James is one of my principal co-operators on the other side. He was commanding a Night Fighting Squadron during the Battle of Britain. He was then, and is now, a very dear friend of mine.

L.L. "Here is a young R.A.F. boy quite unaware of us. Tall, very slim and dark, with big flying boots. James and others are all around him but he can't see them either. Two Guides, one on each side, are directing streams of light on to him from their fingers.

"Now he is beginning to see us. He says he wants to sit down as he is rather tired. He sits down in an armchair. His leg is aching; he takes off one of his flying boots. He says that he 'baled out' and landed badly." (James says No, he never left the machine, but he *thinks* he did.) He speaks: —

" 'Sorry, I can't just make it out. Where am I?' I tell him that he has been brought to me because he can believe what I say.

I show him a photograph to establish my identity. I tell him that we are in Wimbledon.

" 'Thank God Sir! The last I can remember was that we were over the Ruhr. How did they manage to bring me here?' (He thinks it has been done by the underground organisation and is much impressed by its efficiency.)

"I ask him when he left England, and he says Sunday. I tell him this is Thursday. I say that while he has been unconscious he has been brought across a number of frontiers, between Germany and Holland, and between Holland and England, and furthermore that he has crossed the greatest Frontier of all. I hope that this will make him realise what has happened; but not a bit of it, I must try again.

"He asks why he has been brought to we specially; and I say I suppose because I love the boys so much. I never see or hear a big formation going over without saying 'God Bless you and' bring you back safe.'

"He says 'Well, we got back safe all right.' And I say 'Safe.

Yes. Do you know Rupert Brooke's poem called 'Safety'? Let's see if I can remember the last four lines,

"'War knows no power.' Safe shall be my going,
Secretly armed against all death's endeavour.
Safe though all safety's lost; safe where men fall,
And if these poor limbs die, safest of all.'

"He said 'By Jove Sir that's fine. But anyway *I'm* safe.' So I said to him very gently, 'Yes. Safest of all.' That brought it home to him at last. He said, 'd'you mean to say you're trying to tell me that I'm dead?' Then he said 'Why can't you keep still? Why do you keep jumping about?' I replied 'I have already told you that you will see us looking less and less real, and then you will see your friends who have come to meet you. Look round now and tell me if you can see anyone.'

"Then he said 'Hallo. There's Clockie—but how can *he* be here. Clockie's dead.' I said ' He is no more and no less dead than you are.' Then he called out 'Harry!' and added 'Good Lord there's even old Ginger! I must have stumbled into an R.A.F. Camp. I see—I don't mind being dead if this is it, it's a mighty fine piece of work.' Then (answering one of his friends) ' Of course I'm coming. You just try to stop me.'

James: "Thank you Sir. That was well done. He went out from one of the Stations in the South. He was one of our boys. Although you only spoke to one there were six others watching and listening-in. He was the most stable. That was why we chose him as spokesman. His quiet acceptance helped the others. They're a fine lot of boys and we're mighty glad to get them over here; but we think what a poor place Earth is going to be without them."

The third member of our circle said, "Somebody has been trying to make a rabbit out of my handkerchief "and held it up with two knots in the corners. James said "Oh that's Terry; he's always playing the fool instead of getting on with his job!"

The next item from my records is the awakening of an American Red Cross nurse, killed by a German bomb in Italy on the Anzio beachhead.

On the occasion when she was first brought to us L.L, went into trance, and that, as I have explained, always makes things rather more difficult. However, we managed all right, though the conversation shows signs of inanity in places. It doesn't seem to matter very much what one says, so long as one just goes on talking in a matter-of-fact way.

The Guide told us that they were going to bring us a nurse to wake up. It would not be a very difficult job because she had already thought about these things during life.

L.L. went into trance. Then she spoke:

"Oh, it's so hat! it's so hot! They wouldn't bomb a hospital would they? They wouldn't be that mean. There are great big Red Crosses showing. We had just come ashore from a ship. I must get back to the boy or he'll bleed to death. I was fixing a tourniquet. I must take back some more bandages."

I told her that they would be all right in the hospital. She had been brought to me so that I could help her. She must try to compose herself and not worry any more because everything would be all right now. She still complained of the heat, so I asked her if she would like some water; and she drank two glasses with the greatest delight. She said, "Oh, that was lovely water, it's so clear and sparkling, and it hasn't been boiled. All our water is boiled." She clutched the glass tightly with both hands, and I had difficulty in preventing her from spilling it over herself.

Then she noticed the rings on L.L.'s fingers. She noticed particularly one with three stones in it; she said "I wanted one with three stones, but Joe was too poor. He could only give me a ring with one stone. He didn't want me to go to Europe, but I had to go, so I gave him back his ring. He never wrote to me again. Oh, I wish I hadn't sent it back; I do love him so."

About this time she began to realise what had happened to her, and she said, "I've always wanted to wear ear-rings. If this is heaven I shall be wearing ear-rings."

I said "Put up your hand then and see." She put up her right hand and found an earring, but there was none on her left ear. She said "Why, is that an English fashion?" We hunted round and found the other one on the hearthrug. I offered to put it on for her, but she said "Why, no, I guess I can fix it," and did so without difficulty.

She then asked me what the date was, and I told her Feb. 10th. She then asked "What year," and I said 1944. She said "Oh, I'm so glad; I heard that some people stayed unconscious for a long time. It was only on the 3rd that I wrote home." I asked her what her name was, and she said, "Mary, but I guess you'll laugh when I tell you what middle name my Mother gave me. I said, "Well don't tell me if you think I'll laugh at you." She said "No I guess I'll tell you just the same, she called me Mercedes." I said "Well that's a nice name, like a motor car." She said, "Yes, maybe she thought she'd like to have one. But that's what she called me, Mary Mercedes Littlejohn. We lived in Cincinnati." Then she said, "Now I've told you who I am, who are you?" I said, "I expect you've heard of the Battle of Britain, and you may have heard that Sir Hugh Dowding was commanding the Fighters. Well, that's who I am." She said "Gee, ain't that tough, all my life I've wanted to shake hands with an English Lord, and now all I get is a Sir!" I said, "Well it really is rather funny, but since then I have been made a Lord! So if you want to shake hands with a Lord you can shake hands with me!" She took my hand and pumped it up and down, with every appearance of satisfaction.

Then I asked her, "Can't you see anybody else now?" She said "Why yes, I can see such a nice boy. He is in Air Force uniform.

Is he an officer?" I said, "Is he anything like that?" (Taking James' photograph off the mantelpiece). She said "Why yes, that's him." So I effected a ceremonious introduction between her and the invisible James. I asked her if she would go with him," and she said "Why sure I'll go with him." I told her she must put her hair straight before she went, but she said, "It's someone else's hair!" I said, "You must come back and thank L.L. for helping you." She promised to do so, and went off quite happily. L.L. woke up with a start. She said at once that she had an impression that the girl's house in Cincinnati was in 49th Street.

Then James came back and told us that they had got 'six girls from that bombed hospital, but that Mary was the only one ready to wake up. She will wake the others up when they are ready.

She was happy to shake hands. That's what really woke her up, though she didn't really believe that I was a Lord.

On 17/2/44 Mary Littlejohn came back to say "Thank you."

I told her that I had seen in the papers that the Germans hadn't meant to bomb the hospital. A Bomber was being pursued by a British Fighter and jettisoned its bombs. Some of the bullets from the pursuing fighter also fell on or near the hospital.

She said "Oh I don't mind. I'm happy. I don't feel dead. I just wouldn't change if I could. Tell Momma I'm swell. She'll be tickled to death. She doesn't know what has happened yet, but I'll be there when the news arrives."

I chaffed her about not really believing that she had shaken hands with a Lord, and she said "They are all telling me so, so I have to believe it."

She had been taken to the House of Lords when I went there and had seen two new members introduced. The ceremony both amused and impressed her.

She said 'They' were going to bring a lot of Americans to England who, like her, had wanted to come.

She talked about her 'Matron' and said, "Oh I see that my Matron and you are sweethearts" (of course we are, because her Matron is my wife).

James said that "Little Mary" had attached herself to our group of workers.

(On this occasion L.L. was not in trance. The messages came by clairaudience in our normal way.)

I feel bound in honesty to tell you, in connection with this case, that I sent a copy of the two messages to Mrs. Littlejohn, 81, 49th Street, Cincinnati, U.S.A., and that the letter was returned marked 'Unknown.' What slipped up I don't know, but I believe that Little Mary will eventually be vindicated.

June 6th 1944 will go down to history as D-day, when our invasion of Western Europe began. On June 15th we had just finished our healing circle when three soldiers entered the room. L.L. told us: — "Here are three paratroopers. They are quite lost. Talking amongst themselves. One has a Tommy gun strapped to his hip.

One says "I'd give anything for a smoke'."

L.L. "I can't see what they are like. Their faces are a fearful mess (camouflage) and their helmets are right down on their noses. The middle one seems to be an officer."

"I don't think we dare have a smoke. We can't risk striking a match. I wish we knew where we were. What's the use of a map in a fog like this? Talk about a peasouper. Give me old London every time? This is worse than anything I ever knew."

The officer says, "It's damned queer how it came down so suddenly. A lot of things strike me as queer. Generally if it is raining there is no fog; but that grenade went off in a regular downpour, and now look at this! I wonder did we clear them out. It's a funny thing they've disappeared like this."

Now they see Daisy. "Look! A dame."

D. "How are you?"

O. "This is where you practise your French my lad."

2. "She says she can speak English."

O. "Don't trust the woman. She may have a gun on her.

Get round behind her, and if she pulls a gun, let her have it." "You speak English Madame, can you tell us where we are?"

D. " You are in a little house in Wimbledon."

3. " Listen lads, she's nuts."

O. "Can you tell us what part of France we are in?"

D. "I have told you that this is Wimbledon, not France."

2. "I expect she's been to the tennis some time. Ask her if she's hungry."

3. "We can give you some chocolate; we can give you plenty of chocolate. We never want to see any more chocolate in our lives."

O. "Is this a London fog?"

D. "No."

O. "How did we get to be here, are we retreating?"

D. "No, you are not retreating, you have been brought here." Now he sees me and all his suspicions return. He says "If you play any tricks on us we will fill you up with lead." I try him with my photograph to establish identity, but he can't see it.

O. "We want to get to our rendezvous near the river."

Self. "You have crossed the river."

O. "How do you mean we have crossed the river? We didn't cross by a bridge, we didn't swim it and we didn't cross by a boat."

Self. "No, you didn't cross in any of those ways. Did you ever hear of the River Styx?"

O. (Sneeringly). "Oh you're a classical master are you? Look here, we've got to get to a farmhouse with our friends in it. You can show us the way, or we'll lock you in. (Turning to Daisy.) You say you're English. Say 'Peter Piper picked a peck of pickled pepper' and say it fast. Wait till I say GO." Poor Daisy tries and makes a sad mess of it, so I say it for her very fast, and then: — "Now you try. Say 'Hot coffee in a proper copper coffee pot.'" O. Tries, not very successfully.

3. "Hot coffee, Oh for some hot coffee —or hot tea." (To Daisy, pulling at her shoulder) "Could you find us a cup of tea?"

D. (mendaciously) "Yes, certainly.

Now I try another dodge which works sometimes. I go and stand in front of the looking glass and ask O. to come and stand beside me, and ask him what he sees in the glass. He says "I see you." I say "Can't you see yourself?"

O. "No." Self.

"Don't you think that odd?"

O. "Oh I don't know, you see our faces are so well camouflaged."

Self. "I know that your face is very dirty, but that wouldn't prevent your seeing it in the glass, would it?" O. "No I suppose not." But it doesn't penetrate.

3. "I always wanted to go to France when I was a boy. 'La Belle France,' with the lights and the gaiety and the women. And now look at this! France is an awful dull place."

O. "That grenade went off right in front of me and we never so much as turned a hair. I wonder what happened to the Jerries; I'd like to think we cleaned them out. (To D.) Can you show us the way back to the, river?"

D. "I tell you, you are in Wimbledon."

O. "Oh yeah.

I suppose we drifted back across the Channel before the Southwest breeze? Look here, why are you sitting round like this, instead of in comfortable chairs?"

2. "I know Wimbledon. I've been to the tennis, and there is a common with a lake on it. I went there for a picnic once."

O. "Here's a fellow who'll tell us where we are. Here's a fellow in uniform!" (But they lose sight of him again.)

2. "It's a funny thing, but we are inside a house. How did we get in? Did we come through that door? Did it open?"

O. "There's something phony about all this. (To Daisy.) What's the next station down the line from Wimbledon?"

D. "Raynes Park."

O. "What station would you get out at if you wanted to go to the River?"

D. "Kingston." O.

"Can you tell me any places in North London?"

D. Rattles off a string of names.

Self (breaking in). "Look here, you're being pretty rude to this lady. I'll tell you a place in North London.

Stanmore. That was my Headquarters in the Battle of Britain.

I am a retired officer of the Air Force. My name's Dowding. I don't know whether you ever heard it?" For some odd reason, this does the trick. No. 2 comes forward and says, "I know. He's going to tell us that we're dead. The river Styx and all!" Now they can see the 'man in uniform' again.

It is Douglas Hoops, one of the regular Helpers on the other side.

He was killed in a tank battle in North Africa, and his people are engaged in work similar to ours.

O. "Here you are again. Where did you go to?"

D.H. "I've been here all the time, only you wouldn't look at me. Come along with me and I'll get you a nice hot cup of tea."

O. "Thank you."

D.H. " Yes. I expect you'd like to know that you cleaned them out all right. You got them, and they got you. We've got them here too, and you can come along and have a look at them." They go off together, and the last we hear is the voice of No. 3.

"Can we have a smoke, haven't you got a fag?" I expect you noticed how resourceful and well trained the officer was. 'Peter Piper' must be a formidable obstacle to a spy pretending to be English, and his questions on railway stations and localities were shrewd. The idea of taking them off to meet the Germans who had killed them proved useful to me, as you will see from the next extract from my ' Case book.' This deals with a young Londoner killed in Italy. Most of our involuntary guests treat me with a marked lack of the respect which is supposed to be due to grey hairs (not that I mind, bless them!); but Billy was less conspicuously urbane than most, as you will see.

29/6/44
(After the Healing Circle).

L.L. " Here is an infantryman. He calls himself a foot slogger.

He is one of Douglas Hoop's boys. He knows that he's dead, but he won't accept the situation. He is tied to the Earth and doesn't want to try to get loose. Douglas wants us to talk to him and try to get him to move on.

"He is rather short and thickset with a heavy pack and a rifle and thick boots. His name is Billy. He has a nice cheerful face, but it is dirty and unshaven."

B. "This fellow tells me that I'm dead: but I don't want to be dead. I don't want to have anything to do with being dead."

Self. ' 'Don't you want to get rid of that heavy pack? Do you want to keep it always?"

B. "No, Siree! You see I know I was killed, but still I am not dead."

Self. "You feel just the same as ever you did?"

B. "Yes."

Self. "Well, why don't you go along with this chap? He will look after you and give you a fresh start."

B. "I ain't going along with him. He's a fine fellow and he has offered to take me to Piccadilly or Scotland. But I don't want to go to Piccadilly or Scotland. I want to go to the Old Kent Road.

The Old Kent Road on a Saturday night." (Here I make a rather bad mistake.) I say "This fellow will take you to the Old Kent Road." But

Douglas says " No! That's just where I don't want to take him. He has got to break his Earth ties." So I try again.

Self. " You say that you aren't dead."

B. "No. How am I dead? Are you dead?"

Self. "No. But we are alive in different ways." B. "Don't he talk like a doodaw? Yattering like that!" Self. "All right. You are alive. You hit one hand against the other and you can feel it; but you try to hit me. Have you still got your rifle?"

B. "Yes."

Self. "Well, catch me a crack over the head with it."

B. "O.K. You asked for it. (Hesitating.) No. I wouldn't like to do that."

Self. "Well, give me a smack on the back then."

B. (Tries). "How can I when you won't keep still?"

Self. "I didn't move." Then I return to the question of the pack which is encumbering him.

Self. "Why don't you get rid of your pack?"

B. "Because, my dear old cocky, when I want to sleep, I got my ground-sheet, see? And when I want a drink, I got my water bottle, see? You do talk silly; you ought to join the Army, you ought, and get some sense."

Self. "Look here my lad; when were you born?"

B. "1917."

Self. "Very well then; I joined the Army in 1900, 17 years before you were born."

B. " Oh! I thought you talked like one of them sort of blokes."

Self. "Well, anyway, you are not sleepy or thirsty any more now, are you?"

B. "No, I can't say that I am." Then he begins to wonder about the Jerry who killed him and whether he got him too. This opens up a promising line. I say: — "Quick, Douglas, did he get that Jerry? Have you got him over there?"

D.H. "Yes."

Self. "You got that Jerry, and he got you. Why not go with this fellow and have a yarn with him?"

B. "Yes; I'd like to. I'd like to ask him a few things about Concentration Camps; and I'd like to ask him why he didn't throw Hitler out on his ear."

Self. "I expect you'll find that he didn't have very much to do with it. He just went and did what he was told to, like you did."

B. "What do you mean? He had a vote, didn't he? Like. I've got a vote. And next time I vote I'll - No. That's all over now, isn't it?"

Self. "Yes... That's all over. Now you go along with this fellow and find your Jerry and pal up with him. I expect you'll find that he's a very decent chap really." He throws away his rifle and his pack and is ready to go off with Douglas.

D.H. "Really they're surprisingly good fellows. I don't know why I didn't think of looking up Jerry. I don't know what I've let myself in for, but will find him all right." Just a week later, on July 6th, Billy returned.

L.L. "Here's the fellow who went to look for Jerry. He has found him and brought him along."

B. "How are you? I've brought this bloke because he won't believe that I got him." (Douglas Hoops laughs).

L.L. "Billy is going to speak. Jerry is listening. He is so young; he must be under 18. Our answers to Billy will be very important. Jerry doesn't know he has been killed. His name is Heinrich.

"We want him to forget that he was Private So and So. Associate him with youth, his family, the farm, the fields."

B. "I want him to tell us where we are. Just the big town. "

Daisy. "London."

B. "It ain't lying flat, cocky! Lie No. 1 pinned. Have a good look. You people are English, ain't you? You ain't starving.

You ain't scared out of your wits, are you? (To Daisy.) You've had a bit of old Adolf's latest, haven't you? What do you think of Adolf?"

D. "What he is doing doesn't help."

B. " You don't feel bitter? You don't blame the little fellows?"

D. "I think they've been misled."

B. "You don't mind a German soldier coming in here? You got boys in the Army?"

D. "One, in the Air Force."

B. " Ah! I can't tell you what I think of those chaps. That's right. He's getting sense at last. He's seeing now." Heinrich. "Don't you hate me? Wouldn't you torture me? Where do you keep your-arms?"

D. "We haven't got any arms."

H. " The people of England have hid many arms to kill us when we go to England. Even the children would kill us."

D. "We don't want to kill you. Don't you trust anyone?"

H. "I don't trust anyone except the *Herrenvolk*. You say I am in

London—am I a prisoner? No? But there is an English soldier here. He has no gun, but he has been pushing me. He is impolite. All the English are swine. They have no culture.

But he laughs a lot.

"You are like my sister. She has three children. Gretchen, Hans, and the baby. The baby is called Elisabeth for my mother.

"If I am not a prisoner, how did I come to England? My comrades are not here."

"But you are a bad people: you have rained terror from the skies."

B. "Here cocky! Come off it. What you done to us?"

H. "But you are like my sister."

D. "She didn't *hate*, did she?"

H. "You must hate the people who will not set free the enslaved people of Europe. Adolf Hitler will set them free. You are jealous of us. Why does this boy laugh at me?"

Self. "Because you are so funny."

H. "The English have no sense of humour. They are a bad people. God must have made them for His own purpose."

D. "We don't hate you. We are trying to help you."

H. "But you are like my sister. Maybe you have a mother who makes good cheese? You smell the earth when it is newly turned, and it is good. We should get back to, the earth. Why are there so many bad people in the world? "One day—if the Fuehrer does not wish to have it for the Fatherland—I shall own the farm. I am the second son. The eldest was killed in Russia. I am a good farmer. My father was made a cripple by the English in the last war. I am surprised at your kindness. You can't be English."

D. "The Fuehrer has been wrong. He had misled you."

H. "*Heil* Hitler!"

D. "Can't you go back to the farm?"

H. "I'd like to. Four cows are mine. I took them as babies. They were given to me to look after; and now they are four fine fat cows. When I get married I shall have two fields and the four cows. I know a nice girl.

"You are very kind. Perhaps it doesn't matter to make war. It is better to plough. It is better to build a home than to bomb one.

"If this is London, how am I here? You are very strange—all lit up like a lamp. You remind me of my mother on Christmas morning. Her face shines always. (Whispering.) My mother's not like him. Don't tell. (Aloud.) He is a great man, "*Heil* Hitler."

"On Christmas morning we make the cradle with the Baby. *Mein Gott!*" (A flood of tears, and he makes the Sign of the Cross.)

B. "All right lady, he's all right now. He suddenly remembered Christmas. Good enough! We in uniform couldn't get him to forget. Thank you for what you've done. Why is the old bloke writing it all down?"

Self. " I'm doing it to help other people."

B. (To D.) "You're like my mother. She got hers from one of those bombs."

Self. "Aren't you glad to have her with you there?"

B. "I'm thinking of those left behind.

"All three of you look like lamps, lit up. I'll bring him back again to say thank you; that is if this bloke will let me. Calls himself an Officer, but he is only a Corporal; he has Corporal's stripes. Seems to me they can change their stripes whenever they want to."

Self. "He is an Officer. Perhaps he put up Corporal's stripes to make you feel more at ease."

B. "Well! Cheerio folks. Blimey if he ain't writing that down too!"

D.H. "He's all right; he's quite all right. That last burst of emotion gave him sleep and we caught him as he fell. His will be a very beautiful awakening." *

Well, there you are. There are two more souls brought through the grey mists and set on their paths of progress into the Light. There is enmity overcome and brotherhood established.

And don't imagine that ours is the credit for this work. All the time there is a great concourse of bright Spirits collected together at a time suited to our physical convenience, assembled and organised for the help and guidance of the imperishable elements of two insignificant bodies, lying sprawled in the hot Italian sun, and hastily shovelled beneath the surface by a burying party from the advancing army.

Truly the parable of the lost sheep is but a faint example of the love which surrounds every one of the Master's children.

My last story does come under the heading of Rescue Work.

It tells of a man who has sojourned in the Dark Places for 'nearly 300 years of our time.

We had had a warning that a case of special difficulty awaited us, but no indication of what was to come.

L.L. gradually sank into a trance.

---

* On May 26th, 1945, at the Spiritualists' National Union meeting at the Conway Hall, Douglas, Don and Billy returned through the mediumship of Mrs. Helen Hughes. Billy had acquired a piano-accordion, and was playing it while Douglas was talking to his people

Presently a horrible sort of leer spread over L.L.'s face and she began to wash her hands "with invisible soap and imperceptible water," as Gilbert says.

After quite a long time of this she got up out of her chair and spoke to me in a thick indistinct voice in which I only caught the words: Dover Road. Hullo, thought I, a highwayman?

But no. It soon appeared that he was an innkeeper on the old Dover Road and that I was a prospective guest. "You are but plainly dressed Sir for your high position." Then some obsequious and nauseating murmurings about a bed and a wench. "You shall lie soft, my lord, with pillows of the finest down," and then more about the wench.

I took him by the arm (and when I say 'him,' I mean L.L., for he was for the time being in occupation of her body)—I took him by the arm and said sharply "Stop that now and listen to me: you have been brought to me so that I can help you."

(At the back of my mind there was a queer sort of wonder that L.L. should be such a marvellous actress. She was speaking straight out of a historical novel, and I realised the meaning of the expression 'acting the part to the life.')

He threw me off roughly. "I want none of you," he said. He then became violent and incoherent and made rather an ineffectual attempt to strangle me.

I was trying to restrain his struggles as gently as possible so as not to hurt L.L.

"Call on God and on Christ Jesus," I said, "and they will help you."

"God won't help me," he said.

"Yes He will," said I, "He will help every one of His creatures even in the depths of the Pit." And I tried to carry his mind back to his childhood and to the days of his innocence.

He then became violently agitated again: —"Keep these devils off me. Don't let them get at me."

"It's all right," I said, "they won't be able to harm you." Then he collapsed onto his knees on the hearthrug and after swaying about for a few moments, he leant forward, and to my amazement I heard him saying a little baby prayer. I helped him through with the words and then we said it again together.

(Just at this time I noticed in the fire a large black lump of coal, and through two right-angled cracks in it was glowing a perfectly proportioned Sign of the Cross. It persisted for a considerable time and I showed it to the other two after the episode was over.)

Then he knelt upright, and raised his arms towards the ceiling, and cried in a great voice of glad amazement "Why BETSY, BETSY."

I said, "Yes, Betsy has come to meet you. Go with her now and she will look after you."

Then we were given a lovely prayer to the Father "Another of Thy children is rising to Thee"—and the Blessing. Then L.L. sat down and in a few moments was awake again.

She knew nothing of what had happened and only remembered that she had been "Running round with a Cross, holding it up in front of people."

But now comes the sequel.

The following day L.L. was conscious of an interested presence about the house—watching the water coming out of the bath taps, running to the window to watch a trolley bus pass by, examining the electric cooker in the kitchen, etc. Then she was impelled to sit down, and this came through in automatic writing: —

6th day of June 1648.

"I am very grateful to you for your help to me. This is a wonderful country. Though they tell me it is England I know better than to believe them. I have lived in England all my life and I be 64 come next Martinmass.

"I did not like the dark cave I were in last night, and you show me the way out to my Betsy who is my wife who died in childbirth aged 23 years.

"I am Ezra Martin, owner of the Dun Cow, famous for its ales.

I was a bad man after my Betsy die, but we are here, my Betsy and me, my Betsy who die" (the writing trailed away).

Then one of the Guides spoke in explanation. "He has realised now what has happened to him. That is why we wanted him to write. We showed him this earth of yours, and its wonders amazed and delighted him. Now it is time he realised that he is in a new world never to face death again. His wife was helped and asks us to thank you all for your help. We do most heartily." "Ezra Martin had murdered five travellers by smothering them in their beds. The last of them has now forgiven him, and not until then could he be liberated."

Now I don't want you to think that there is anything unique in what we are doing. It is going on all over the country. One man wrote and told me that he had been doing it for 25 years now, and I know a little old lady in Devon, very simple, and very poor in this world's goods, who has classes of spirits brought her to teach. She reads them little Bible stories, like a Sunday school—as children they listen to words they have never heard before, and as little children they rise again towards the Light which they have spurned.

I have no doubt that among my readers are many who are also doing this unobtrusive but blessed work. For indeed it is a blessed work. It is the work of our Lord and Master—it is the work of the Christ Spirit which lies at the root of every great religion in the world.

You may say "Why don't the great Saints and Angels do this work? Why is it left to poor fallible mortals to influence the destinies of the dead?"

I reply, "I don't know *why*. Who am I to explain the work of the Great Ones? I only know that there is some quality in our human earthly vibrations, if they be of love, which is needed to complete the great Spiral of God's Power when it is used in the astral regions close to the Earth.

I only know that we *can* help the dead, by our prayers, by our thoughts, by our love.

I know that the loving thought which burns a candle to the dead in a Catholic Church is not lost; though it is the love and the thought and the prayer, and not the candle, which avails. Why do we Protestants stand coldly aside and leave our dead to shift for themselves, so far as we are concerned, when we could do so much to help them? I say that the poor souls wandering in the mists, the poor earthbound souls, aye and the poor souls working out their own Salvation in the Age Long Darkness, stand in bitter need of our love and prayer. And there is no soul or spirit so high that he does not gain an added grace and blessing from our humble prayers—though, indeed, in thus giving we receive far more than we give.

CHAPTER VIII

PSYCHIC HEALING

Now I must deal with a question of Psychic Healing. This is, for me, the most difficult chapter in the book, for a variety of reasons.

In the first place, most of my knowledge has been obtained at second-hand and I cannot vouch for it from personal experience.

Secondly, there is an extreme variety of method in existence, and my summary may not therefore be comprehensive. And thirdly, it is difficult to adduce proof in individual cases.

When absent treatment has been followed by a cure, it often happens that neither the patient nor the doctor knows that any other influence has been at work, and there is always the question of 'post hoc' or 'propter hoc?' which may very pertinently be asked.

Again, while doctors as a whole are far more open-minded than the clergy or scientists in psychic matters, it is simply not fair to press a doctor to give his testimony if he is reluctant to do so. His practice is his living and, quite apart from the Big Stick of the British Medical Association in the background, his other patients may take fright if he acquires a reputation for lack of orthodoxy.

Here, if I may do so without offence, I should like to pay a tribute to the progressiveness of the Church of England in this particular respect. The late Archbishop of Canterbury set up a Committee to inquire into a report upon the subject of Divine Healing. The Chairman is the Bishop of Croydon and the Archbishop's representative is Mr. Godfrey Mowatt, a vehicle of great experience in Spiritual Healing, and, while I have no authority to forecast the line of action which his present Grace will follow when he receives its report, I have little doubt that the main tenor, at least, of its findings will reach the public in due course.

Mr. Mowatt's method of working is on the highest level. He dislikes being called a Healer, and represents himself as a channel only. He emphasises the need for the Healer to cast out every thought of Self, and he makes the point that, even in cases of apparent failure, healing of the Spirit may have been effected, Which is infinitely more important than healing of the body.

After some thought I have decided not to attempt, myself, to quote any individual cases of healing. For those who ask for chapter and verse, there are books galore. From among these I may mention *Parish the Healer* by Maurice Barbanell. Psychic Press Ltd., 144, High Holborn, *Experiences in Spiritual Healing* by an East Anglian Farmer. W, E. Harrison & Sons, The Ancient House Press, Ipswich, and *The Living Touch* by Miss Dorothy Kerin, Chapel House, Mattock Lane, Ealing.

But almost every Spiritualist Church and Home Circle will have its own experiences to relate to the genuine inquirer, though methods will be widely different.

How different these methods are, I will now endeavour to indicate; and I ask pardon in advance for the inadequacy of my presentation. I must also point out that two or more methods may overlap in any particular case.

1. Prayer, followed by the Laying on of Hands. This is perhaps the highest form of Spiritual Healing. Seers have observed Spirit hands reinforcing the efforts of the human operator. .
2. X-Ray sight for diagnosis, followed by normal medical treatment. The medium sees the actual growth or lesion and describes it to the doctor.
3. Spirit diagnosis, followed by normal medical treatment.
4. Spirit diagnosis, followed by manipulation or other action by the medium.
5. Spirit diagnosis, followed by spirit prescription for pharmaceutical treatment.
6. Spirit diagnosis, followed by colour or light treatment.
7. Absent treatment with or without the knowledge of the patient and/or doctor.
8. Absent treatment (physically considered). The medium in his Astral Body visits the patient.

9. Healing by virtue of spiritually charged waters. (As at Lourdes).
10. Actual manipulative surgery by means of materialised spirit-hands.
11. Magnetic healing, in which the spiritual element is apparently absent, though this absence may be more apparent than real.

Now if I were a family doctor, I should certainly be horrified on reading the above list. I should be reminded of the story of a General Practitioner who got a telephone call just as he was sitting down to dinner. He at once rushed out and started putting on his coat. His wife asked, "What's the matter, dear?" "It's from Mrs. Jones about her little boy."

"What has happened to him? "

"He has cut his finger."

"Well, surely you needn't rush off like this; you can finish your dinner first."

"No I can't. Mrs. Jones has got a book called *What to do before the Doctor Comes*; and I want to get there before she does it."

The number of Psychic Healers in this country is increasing everyday, and not all are on the same level of selflessness and efficiency. It is this problem with which the Archbishop's Committee is largely concerned, and it is a thorny problem indeed. For the Healer who takes it upon himself to interfere by advice or action with the treatment prescribed by a qualified Doctor is incurring a grave responsibility, and may render himself liable to legal prosecution. Perhaps the less said on this difficult subject the better, pending the results of the labours of the Committee afore-mentioned.

But it is obvious that psychic diagnosis and treatment carried out in conjunction and cooperation with the medical profession cannot be subject to criticism; and many of the methods mentioned above are unobjectionable, provided that the patient has not been urged to discontinue professional treatment nor to ignore medical advice.

Running through my list again, nobody I think is likely seriously to object to the "laying on of hands": the worst that the materialist could say of it is that it is useless.

Items No. 2 and 3 presuppose cooperation with, and the assent of, the medical profession.

Nos. 4, 5 and 6 are the types of treatment where the medium must use special care not lightly to offend against established practice, unless a case has been abandoned as hopeless by the Doctors.

Nos. 7 and 8 cannot logically be condemned by a legal system which adopts as a basic principle the attitude that Spirit communication is impossible.

No. 9 seems all right. I haven't heard yet of anyone being prosecuted for making a pilgrimage to Lourdes.

No. 10. I can well imagine a quite frenzied opposition to manipulative surgery carried out by Spirit hands. The difficulties attending the launching of a successful prosecution, however, will be obvious.

No. 11. About magnetic healing I shall have more to say in this chapter. At the moment it will suffice to point out that this aspect of the healing art is (ostensibly) free of the stigma of Spirit contamination, and so may perhaps tempt materialists to investigate some of its remarkable phenomena; phenomena which are open to investigation by 'scientific' methods. By which I mean to say that they can be indefinitely repeated under laboratory conditions, and measured by counting revolutions with a stopwatch and balancing forces on a measured scale.

But before embarking on this theme I think I ought to give you some idea of the work of our own little healing circle. I write with some diffidence on the subject, because I only dimly understand what we are doing. We are not the healers; we only contribute our quota of power at the earth wavelength to mingle with the higher vibrations and create the mixture which is used for healing purposes.

The procedure, as I understand it, is as follows. We give to the Healers the name of a sick person, and the Healers examine the aura and the etheric body. Any condition of ill health is shown by a colour-deficiency in one or both of these vehicles. We are then told what to do, and we are taught to build up simultaneously the strongest colour-thought form of which we are capable.

It may, for instance, be a beam of light, or a spiral in which the patient stands, or a coloured rain like the sparks from a firework, or a hood, or a fabric in which the defective part is wrapped. The colours most often used are gold, or silver, or green, or yellow, or dark or light blue, or rose-colour. The treatment restores the deficient colour to the etheric body and that acts upon the physical body—not instantaneously, but after a lapse of time which may run into months.

This work has made me realise one thing very vividly, and that is that the words 'Thought is real' are not a mere meaningless cliché. On the contrary thought is quite surprisingly appreciable. On one occasion we were told to imagine an injured knee being wrapped in a white shimmering material. L.L. said, "Someone is thinking of the material being wrapped round and round and round. The knee needs only to be enveloped loosely in the fabric." This was quite true. I had been imagining the material being applied like a bandage wrapped round and round the knee.

On another occasion we were visualising a shining silver ball, and L.L. said, "No, no, Daisy, you're thinking green. Think bright sparkling silver." Daisy said that she had in fact been visualising one of those Christmas tree ornaments which have a distinct tinge of green.

It all sounds a bit crazy, I know; and it is not always effective so far as we are able to see, but most of the cases appear to benefit from the process, and in some the results are electrifying.

I am not in a position to prove that anything has happened which could not be explained by coincidence; but I am sure that we have never harmed anyone and I firmly believe that in perhaps 25% of our 'cases' cures have been effected which would not have taken place without our intervention.

As I say, I write with considerable diffidence upon this subject, but I did not think it fair to write a chapter on psychic healing and omit all description of our own experience, limited though it has been.

To revert now to the subject of magnetic healing. I expect that some of you have thought that I have been making an unwarranted assumption when speaking of the 'etheric body,' or the etheric counterpart of the physical body. If I tell you that this body provides the ectoplasm out of which materialisations are built up, you remain unimpressed because you have never seen materialisation and possibly do not want to.

Now I tell you that this etheric body is continuously exuding its substance from the finger-tips or toes of the physical body, and that this substance is physical (that is to say, it does not long survive the physical body) although it exists in a gap between the gaseous state and the ultimate physical atom, a gap of which scientists are hitherto ignorant.

You say, "Prove it," and I reply "You can prove it for yourself with the homeliest of materials."

Take a strip of paper about 8.5 inches long and 3 inches wide (the exact dimensions are immaterial, but the paper should be fairly stiff and preferably rough-surfaced) and gum the ends together so as to form a cylinder 3 inches deep and about 2.5 inches in diameter.

Pierce the cylinder as near as possible to its upper rim and pass a stiff straw through from side to side: take care that the straw passes through the axis of the cylinder, or it will be lopsided: cut the ends of the straw off short. Now push a small needle down through the straw at its middle point and at right angles to its length: the point of the needle should protrude about 0.5 inch below the lower side of the straw. Now get a thin medicine bottle and stand it upside down on a table, and set the point of the pin in the centre or the glass bottom of the bottle.

You will now have your cylinder balanced on a practically friction-less pivot and free to revolve under the slightest impulse.

Cup one of your hands round the cylinder with the fingers horizontal, but without touching it, and the cylinder will begin to revolve. If it doesn't revolve for the right hand, it will for the left.

Now if you put the bottle and cylinder in the middle of the room on a small table round which you can easily move, you will find that the direction in which you are facing makes a considerable difference, and if (for instance) you get the maximum rotation with your right hand when facing East, that will be the direction of minimum rotation for the left hand; whereas, if you change round and face West, you will get the maximum rotation for the left hand and the minimum from the right.

This opens up a new line of thought; because it would seem that not only is something coming out from your fingers which is sufficiently substantial to make the cylinder revolve, but that' something' is kindred in its nature to another 'something' which varies with the points of the compass.

A later development has been that the cylinder can be made to revolve, without any human influence, under the impulse of that 'something' in the atmosphere, in suitable conditions (i.e. when the 'current' is flowing strongly). It is only necessary to shield the East or West half of the cylinder, with a semi-cylindrical screen of tin or cardboard or glass, so that the current can operate on the exposed half only.

If you play a little with this toy, I think that you will soon convince yourself that draughts, or the warmth of your hands, cannot account for the motion, although the former have of course to be guarded against. The maximum rotation which I have generated in this crude apparatus is about 40 revolutions per minute. This was obtained in both directions with a cylinder made of paper in which I had stabbed a multitude of holes with a pin, in order to increase its surface roughness. The cylinder can be 'made to revolve, by the influence of the screen, under a draught-proof cellophane cover.

This is not the only evidence concerning the emanations from the human fingers. There is an apparatus known as the Kilner screen by means of which this outflow, and the human aura, can be seen. Those interested can obtain further details from The London Psychic Educational Centre, 17, Ashmere Grove, Acre Lane, London, S.W.2.

The greatest investigator of animal magnetism was probably Baron von Reichenbach. His book was translated and edited by Professor Gregory of Edinburgh University and published in 1850 under the short title of *Reichenbach on Magnetism*. I imagine that it must now be practically impossible to obtain.

He dealt with magnetism and magnetic emanations in all forms, using as his instruments persons having cataleptic tendencies. Such persons are apparently able to see magnetic flames and emanations with comparative ease in the absence of other light.

Unfortunately for his life's work, his book was published at about the time when Faraday gave to the world the results of his researches in Electro-Magnetism. The practical value of the latter was so great that the labours of Reichenbach appear to have attracted little attention—in this country at least. Nevertheless, no serious student of the subject can afford to overlook his work.

It seems reasonable to suppose that some part (though perhaps the least important) of the effect of the Laying on of Hands may be derived from this material substance which flows from the fingers.

Truly the barrier between the physical and the spiritual is thin indeed.

My next item for the attention of scientists is equally attractive to the amateur experimentalist. It is the practical application of a tiny aspect of the budding science of Radiesthesia.

Of the general subject I have space only to say that it begins with the art of the Water Diviner, and extends into a multiplicity of branches of magical interest. Its principal apparatus is the pendulum, held in the human fingers. Gypsies have long used a gold ring suspended from a hair to determine the sex of eggs or chicks.

Get a gold signet ring, or some other small object of approximately that weight, and fasten it onto 3 or 4 inches of silk or dental floss.

Hold this silk between your finger and thumb pointing downwards and hang the ring just above a tablet of saccharin. You will soon see if you are one of the people for whom the pendulum will' work.' (It will work for most people.) Then you can try it over Aspirin and Vitamin B. and strong poisons, and photographs and see what different results you get. I can't deal with that now. I have only introduced you to the subject of a lifetime's experiment.

But if the pendulum will work for you, then try this. Take an ordinary piece of string about 4 yards long, without any knots, and lay it out on the floor. As might be supposed, the pendulum hangs over it inertly. Now take an electric wall-plug out from its socket, take one end-of the string and tie it on to both terminals of the plug, and push the plug back into its socket.

The effect then is that you have short-circuited the terminals, but with a non-conductor, so that no current flows in the inch or so of string which lies between the terminals, still less can any current be flowing in the rest of the string which is still lying loose on the floor.

But hang the pendulum over the string now, and it will begin to swing across the line of the string. There is SOMETHING in the string which was not there before. That 'something' is not electric current, nor is it electro magnetism, because it won't deflect a compass needle.

Now tie the loose end of the string round your ankle and read a book for 5 or 10 minutes. Then try the pendulum again. It hangs motionless. (I know I ought not to say what the pendulum will do with you. I ought to confine myself to saying that that is what it does with me. Sorry.) Go on with your book for another half hour or so, and try again. The pendulum has come to life again, but this time it is swinging along the string instead of across it.

Now, so far, nobody can take much objection to what I have said. I have merely described some results which have followed causes in experiments which I have made. You may find that the same results do not follow your own imitation of my procedure, and you may conclude that I have been deceiving myself or am trying to deceive you. In either case no great harm has been done.

But now I am going to be much more rash. I am going to say that I believe that the 'something' in the string goes into the body (probably the etheric body) and acts as a magnetic healing agent for certain diseases. Try it for half an hour night and morning, on a gouty knuckle, and see if it does for you what it has done for me.

I know two doctors who use this on themselves, though wild horses would not draw from me their names.

That is all I propose to say on the subject at present, except that there lies ahead of the methodical experimentalist in this field the possibility of making discoveries of worldwide importance; and that without elaborate and expensive apparatus, but with paper and pins and string, and the homely tools which are found in every household.

CHAPTER IX

DREAMS AND SLEEP

N ow for a chapter on work during Sleep. You may remember that in the early part of Chapter VII Denis said to me, "If people knew what you do in sleep, they would indeed say you were crackers." And now I must tell you, and submit to the soft impeachment.

The amazing thing is that I never have the slightest vestige of an idea of what has been happening. So far as I am aware I spend the time dreaming about entirely different things, confused and ridiculous things, things which are too silly even to raise a laugh at the breakfast table, things which cannot be twisted by my utmost ingenuity into any relation with what I may afterwards be told that I have been doing.

While, therefore, I feel that I know that the other recorded incidents in which I have participated are true, I have no such innate conviction as regards the sleep adventures which I am about to relate.

Nevertheless I firmly *believe* them to be true, or I should not risk my residual reputation for sanity by telling you about them.

This is from Clarice: —

> You were with me last night. We took four little boys from the 'sick bay' of the hospital to the playroom in the children's home. They were four little children who had left their parents behind, and they were a little afraid. We couldn't seem to quieten one little boy.

"Then the Egyptian friend who has helped me so much said you might try. You stood there, oh, how I smiled, so shy and diffident, wondering what you could do. Then, to our surprise, you changed your etheric robe into an Air Force uniform. We none of us thought you could do that. You are full of surprises.

"As soon as the child saw your uniform he ran to you and said, 'My daddy is in the Air Force, too.' He was quite at ease after that and went with us quite happily. You left him with the other children, and he did not notice our going. That was a good job of work.

That was in early June 1943, when a number of children had been killed in a daylight raid on a South Coast church.
And now here is Z. in October 1943: —

"Last night was a night of activity on the lower planes. You are a restless person and always anxious to be with your flying steeds. Last night you and I went with a Formation, and you led the Invisible Brothers who intercept the explosions and save many an earth life. They are very foolhardy, these flying warriors, and often swoop low even when the air is reverberating with shock.

Often they would suffer from the repercussions, if their invisible brothers did not deflect the vibrations.

"I myself have watched them say, 'Thought we should have felt that one,' flying so low!' They did not realise that they would not have felt anything again if they had been left to themselves.

"What does this name mean which I see so often with them— WHOOPEE?" (I explain.) "It is always accompanied by an uplift of spirit. It is a word of power, and very often used. I wondered if it was some god they worshipped, because it brought with it no figure, only sound.

"That is what you were doing last night and then you went to Heartsease's garden where we discussed what you should say, and where we decided to give more time to your young friend James.

James goes sometimes for refreshment to Heartsease's home. She entertains many from the company of warriors, because she says that they are her boys, too!' "You will know henceforth, what you are doing with us. Every big formation which goes out automatically draws you the moment you leave the earth body.

"You may think it strange that we should need your help so much. Here is the reason.

"We are working in the Shadowland between the Earth and the lower heavens. There, hundreds of these young men are remaining voluntarily, that they may help their comrades still in the flesh.

To them we appear very often as remote personages, to be followed with a kind of religious zeal—leaders who are a little out of touch —though they are quite unaware of this attitude themselves.

"When they recognise one who is familiar and whom they trust, they surge forward with such a tremendous impetus that they carry all before them. They know that they have passed the first death, and the majority of them think that you have also. That does not matter. All that matters is that they can follow you.

"It is not only my love for you which makes me work with you, but the great love which binds us to Him, and the opportunity to forward His plan. Truly He sees all, and weaves a wondrous pattern." On another occasion Clarice came and told me that on the previous night I had been working in Concentration Camps, bringing sleep to sufferers. Afterwards, she told me, she took me to the Animal Sphere. "Don't you remember?" (No.) "Don't you even remember the little fawn which followed you about?" Alas, no. I was busy having a horrible nightmare.

Clarice said, "I do wish you could remember. Each time you go back you say you are sure you will remember this time. But you never do." Next I should like to tell you about the Star which the boys gave me. (This wasn't in sleep, but it fits in.) A number of R.A.F. boys grouped together. Peter is acting as spokesman. He comes forward and places round my neck a deep mauve ribbon by which is suspended a lovely 'medal,' shining like crystal. It is more like a light above my heart.

"It is presented by the boys over here for all that you are doing to ease the sorrow of those whom they love. You see we are having an

---

* They call Clarice 'Heartsease' over there.

79

Honours List too." (I thank him and them.) They are formed up in the shape of a star and are standing now behind Z. who has just turned towards us. There is a star of R.A.F. boys and wings of sailors and soldiers, rather in the shape of the R.A.F. badge.

Z. "Greetings to you my brother. It rejoices me to take part in this little celebration of which Love is the keynote. That star which has been presented to you is an emblem representing two things—First of all Him whom we all serve, and secondly (so those who have given it to you inform me) that to which they aspired; 'towards the stars" (I explain the meaning of the Air Force motto, *Per Aruba ad Astra*. Through hardship towards the stars.) "How fitting! Knock off the last letter. Through hardship towards the Star. The Star which shines so clearly at this time.

Oh my brother, could we but inflame the hearts of men that they would go forward in zeal to clear away all the mists which lie between them and this Star. Could they but glimpse one sparkling point, and accept it and hold it, how much easier would be their load.

"Since last it shone forth in splendour, you have worked with us to bring a little of its light more clearly before men, and now as it shines forth again, we thank you in His Name. And, as those who love you have created for you a replica of His symbol, so we, who have watched them, bring from Him, and infuse into that star which shall forever glow upon your heart, His Love.

"And now may His Blessing rest upon you all; may you go forward strong in His work; may you be deemed worthy to feel His Presence and be glorified therein. And unto Him shall all men aspire, and unto Him shall be brought all who are weak, all who labour and all who sorrow, that He may take them in His arms and bring them peace. Amen."

Clarice. "I was at the party! I made the ribbon which held the Star. This is a real ribbon, I made it out of real things, and when you come here it will be real to you. We wanted to mark a year of movement. James suggested that you deserved a medal, but he didn't know what kind, so he asked Z. He said that the Star was the highest that could be given.

"The Star was made by the boys; not only of the Air Force but of all the Services, because it is not only your boys that you have helped. They fashioned the Star.

"For the ribbon we chose mauvy pink. Purple of royalty and pink of love, but Z. took the ribbon and Star to be blessed, only he could have done that: so you see we've all had a hand in it.

"That's one thing that you will be able to bring with you when you come over here." Now let's talk about somebody else for a change. I want to tell you a very strange thing; which is that living people, in sleep, not only work alongside those who inhabit the Astral and higher Spheres, but they sometimes carry out the work of meeting those who are killed in action and helping them across the Valley of the Shadow of Death.

Here follow three episodes of work over the sea, carried out by women living in England now. I have given them their next-life frames so as to avoid embarrassment. The stories are related by Amore. (I should explain that the group which is employed on this work is much larger than our own little circle, though we are all members of it.)

Amore. In the Pacific. Out over the sea. Very calm and lovely. Someone clinging to a piece of driftwood. A young boy; fair complexion. He lets go the driftwood and comes rushing up to meet me so gladly.

"I always knew my angel would save me." As I gather him into my arms, I am suddenly aware that I have great wings. He is content and quiet.

"Is this dying?"

"Yes, there's your body down there."

"I'm not sorry to leave it; it was pretty well smashed up. These filthy Japs—don't—don't drop me."

"All right, but forget the Japs. I'm not strong in hate."

"O.K. Gee, I'm glad I wasn't too bad. Guess mum will be upset though. I'm her only son. Where are you taking me?"

"Somewhere to rest. You are tired."

"Not now I'm not. Axe all these angels carrying just-dead people like me?" (I was aware that all the band of workers looked like angels.) "Yes. Each has someone."

"Gee, God is good."

The great violet ray enfolded us as he spoke, and he slept. I left him in the Home of Rest. Koos asked me to go back to the sea.

"It's rather a difficult task. If you need help send for me." Over the sea again. A distress signal flashed. Down I went.

"You're blinding me!" a voice cried in agony. I drew my cloak closely round me. Yora was battling with a man, a submarine officer. Her cloak had slipped and her light shone into his face.

I readjusted it for her, he couldn't see me.

"Thanks Amore, he's terribly afraid."

"German?" "Yes and not too savoury."

"Do you need help?"

"Link up with the Master of Love. He's so afraid, poor fellow."

We thought of the Great Ray and gradually he stopped struggling and grew quiet.

There's my case—an airman tangled in a wrecked plane under the water. The water-people help me. He is asleep, but as I touch him he awakes.

"For God's sake Babs, go away. I've told you I'm finished.

You should have taken care."

"I'm not Babs."

"Oh! Muriel. Look dear, these things don't last indefinitely.

Honestly I'm not worth a tear."

"I'm not Muriel."

"Then who the hell are you? Gad, I should have stuck to wine. Phyllis, just one kiss. In these days a girl has to march with the times."

"I'm not Phyllis; you must come with me."

"Why? Oh-why did I chase that Jerry? I should have been back at Base by now instead of in this filthy water—water—water.

Hey you! Where are you? What d'you want to disappear for? Why am I able to breathe in the water?"

"Because you are dead."

"Dead! Pull another one. I wouldn't be talking to you if I was dead."

"Neither would you be able to breathe under water."

"God! If you're right. Then these spiritualistic people who talk to spooks are right. You don't die."

"Only the body dies."

"Then we can get away from here?"

"Certainly, take my hand."

"Look here sister, no monkey business. I don't carry money or anything of value on these trips. "

"I don't want money."

"Then what the hell do you want?"

"To take you home."

"Home! That's a good joke. Do you know where my home is? Blown to blazes. My wife and kid too. He was just sixteen months old. God damn and blast every filthy swine of a Hun." The wave of hate and darkness surged over me. I felt faint, but remembered to open my cloak so that he could see my light. As he cursed and swore I kept struggling with the darkness. He wouldn't move. "I can't see. I can't see. "Oh God! What have I done to deserve this?"

"Can't you see me? I'm still here."

"No. I can't see anything. Christ help me!" A flash of light cast the darkness away as he cried the Blessed Name, and I knew suddenly what to do. I changed my features.

"Can you see me now?"

"Bubbles, Bubbles darling; they didn't get you after all! Darling, darling, hold me, I'm falling." As he lost consciousness I caught him and bore him to the Home of Rest. Koos met me. "You managed? Splendid! His wife is just ready to wake up. He'll see her when he is rested. Go to the Garden now, you need rest."

My next story is an account of my last Birthday Party. Clarice had said: —

"We'll have a very special party the night before your birthday." Next week I told her that, as usual, I hadn't been able to remember anything about it.

Clarice. "It was a splendid party and very well organised.

All the best people were there. The party was held in the garden.

The children decorated the trees with flowers. Now the flowers here are different from yours—they are alight. You would have to put little lights in your flowers, ours are luminous in themselves.

"We had races. The children and the animals raced. And games—oh a lovely party! There were groups of children who have recently come over; little ones who have died from starvation. We made your party theirs and gave them everything they had ever dreamed of having, and it was all so real to them.

"Do you know what they called you? 'Uncle Bright.' They're not quite used to the luminous quality in us yet. Then, after you had been away working and had come back, we had our orchestra play for you. One of our R.A.F. friends set to music words I had often seen in your heart, and the children sang them. That's what we wanted you to bring back—that and the sound of the orchestra.

The words were 'The Lord is my shepherd, I shall not want'." James. "I just want to wish you many happy returns too, and also to tell you that a great number of boys are coming over to us and we don't have to tell them anything. They're quick in the uptake. Do you know why? Because they've read your book, and they want you to know that, while they admired you on earth, nothing but a deep love can ever repay what you've given to them in helping them to realise just what has happened.

"We think you ought to know about it. They're coming over fast Sir, but they're coming over knowing. Some got the book because you had written it and got the shock of their lives when they opened it. But it's helped them. We only wish there were more of them about, because sometimes we know who is coming over, and we just shove it under their noses." Talking of birthdays, I was speaking to Clarice on my father's birthday and I said to her "give Dad a little kiss from me for his birthday." She said "Give him one yourself. Here he is." So I said tactlessly "Many happy returns Dad." With deep feeling he replied "God forbid that I should return."

And now I will finish this chapter with a story from the jungle. Burma? Malaya? Indo-China? What do I know?

The date is February 1st, 1944. L.L. is speaking: —

"Steamy jungle. Hordes of workers everywhere. Our band was moving swiftly towards a group of men working in the swamp.

They were piling bricks and rubbish on top of each other, layer after layer, between stakes. (Were they building a toad?) They were working slowly and wearily. A guard, a Jap, was walking up and down along a strip of solid ground, and every now and then he would take his bayonet and strike out at a worker. The workers were up to the waist in the swamp, and looked like animals with long matted beards and bleary eyes and matted hair falling down over their faces. (Can these be white men?) "I hurried to a man who was gasping for breath as he struggled to carry a long pole towards the road. He fell on his face and staggered up again, still holding the pole. The guard leapt on him and beat him with the butt of his bayonet so that he fell in the mud again. As he rose, the Jap turned his bayonet and plunged it into the man's back.

"I felt that thrust, and a swift surge of anger overcame me. I rushed at the Jap, but was helpless as he plunged the bayonet into the man.

"I felt mad with anger and impotence, but was unable to move, though I wanted to go to the man. Suddenly Hugh was beside me and he laid his arm round my shoulders. 'Don't think of it,' he said, 'this man needs you.' "Immediately I felt calm again and went to the man whom Hugh was supporting. He gave him to me with a smile.

"I took the poor soul to Chang's home of rest. Chang sent him off in charge of one of the workers and told me to follow him.

We went into a long spacious room. A man was working with some large coloured bulbs.

"I lay down on a low couch, and the man turned a lovely blue globe towards me. I was bathed in a glorious peace...

"Back in the swamps, I saw that the groups were working hard.

Hugh with a group of five which I joined was concentrating on the men who were working. The star on his breast was gleaming and expanding into a great light. It was as though all his own light and that of the others were concentrated in it. The beam turned out towards the men and enveloped them. The word we all held was Endurance.

"Another group was concentrating on the guards a soft rosy glow, the Love Ray. From time to time others reinforced this group.

"The whole atmosphere was foul and heavy. I felt weighted down by a terrible depression and agony. It was this vibration we were trying to dispel. All around in the undergrowth I was conscious that dark slimy creatures were lurking. A stench rose to my nostrils. I felt so terribly unclean, and only by concentrating on Hugh, who was calmly sending the beam from his star onto the labouring men, could I keep conscious.

"Later, in the Hall of Learning, the Teacher spoke earnestly on the great need for concerted effort in the direction of Love and Mercy. Only a small minority of the earth people understand and are consciously working for Unity and Love. That the few who try to stem the flood of darkness must be constantly on the alert, sparing no effort to bring the light.

"As we took our places for the blessing, I saw for the first time that below us there were rows and rows of people who did not look up as the Light shone out. I knew that these are the people we are pledged to help. The light encompasses them, but they are unaware, just as before I was unaware of their presence."

The next instalment of the story came about a week later. Z is speaking: —

"Now I would remind you of the work we accomplished last night. With your little group you went into a condition on the earth where hatred was rife, where men have become even less than the animals, where passion and despair hold many in their grip. Some there were who were being tortured—helplessly held; others were forced to witness this, helpless to alleviate the pain. To each one of those crucified went one of the band and helped them to endure, taking to themselves the residue of pain which the poor mortal frame could not bear. You understand -that each one had to bear to the uttermost and those who helped could only shoulder a small part.

"When the spirits were free and those misguided—oh so sadly straying from the path—those wretched creatures turned to find others upon whom to work their will, then did the real battle begin. For with the strength of your own high purpose and unselfish love you did battle with the lusts and passions of these miserable creatures, and by a mighty concentration of will-power and love, so sickened their hearts within them that the desire to inflict pain passed from them. I wish, how I wish, I could say passed from them forever; but alas it is only a temporary respite and all of you must do battle again. That is the work in which we can only watch lovingly, the redemption of Mankind lies in Man.

"Here is a special task which you have accepted and which I now bring to your consciousness.

"You will night and morning, with all the power at your command with all the will of which you are capable, with all the love that you ever hope to experience, engage in personal conflict with these the Grey People, that their hearts shall sicken within them, and that feeble flicker—oh so feeble—of the Divine Light shall flare up. It is the only way. Love shall transmute Hate. Beauty shall replace ugliness, and men shall remember their true estate.

"Think not that, because physically you are unaware of the conflict, you are not taking part. Without your Star the little band would indeed work in darkness."

Three weeks later Chang told us that our work with the Grey People had had some effect, and James told me that the camp in the swamp had been moved. He said "The poor chaps aren't much better off, but at least they are on dry land now."

I pass now to another instalment of the Night Record on 5th of April.

"I became aware of the group already at work in the jungle. Two Japanese were drawing water from a well. Near them were standing two men holding buckets—tins with rope as handles.

"The soldiers were arguing. One was urging that the white men should be allowed to draw water too: the other that they should take it from a muddy stream near by. Hugh took three of us and we went and stood round the Jap who was urging clear water and thought hard to encourage him while Hugh turned his mind to the other. Gradually No. 2 moved away and No. 1 waved the two shaggy-bearded men to take water.

"The men took their tins and filled them and then bent down and drank. One even swilled his hands and face and the Jap turned his back.

"'God, that's good,' the man turned and grinned at his companion, and they started to walk up a narrow path. Hugh followed and waved us on, Came to a camp. The water-carriers were hailed with jokes and laughter which turned to satisfaction as the water was passed round. There was not enough for all.

"Two of us stood behind the men as they asked for more. Hugh kept closely linked with the Jap. Permission was granted and the men went off with two guards.

"The men in the camp were gaunt and bearded, but very cheerful. They were discussing the new guard. One man said 'All we want is a good wash.'

" 'The age of miracles isn't over' remarked another, 'witness two tins of clean drinking water.'

"Hugh moved off with two helpers. We others carried on, drawing the waves of laughter up and strengthening them and returning them to the men ... It was like taking fine threads of silver and weaving them into a thin gauze which the auras of the men absorbed.

"Presently the Jap came back and spoke to the men. They moved off a few at a time.

"Became aware of James. He was laughing. 'Trust the Chief to get them their bath.'

"Chang was smiling too, and told me it was time to return to the Hall of Learning. Hugh joined us, very cheerful and pleased with himself. ' I even got them to produce some soap,' he said.

"James told us that this is the camp we have been working at for some time."

Well, that is the story. Call it a fairy story if you like, but I like to think that some fairy stories are true, and that this is one of them.

Perhaps one day, when the Boys come marching home, some released prisoner may recognise the incidents—who knows?

CHAPTER X

JAMES

I feel that I have now finished all that I can usefully say about the work of our circle as outlined at the end of Chapter III. The last three items do not lend themselves to description.

As regards the improvement of our education, that is going on all the time and will (I hope) persist indefinitely. The contributions of power which we make when so required are intrinsically impossible to describe, even if that were permissible; and there is little to be said about the literary work - that must be judged on its merits.

My plan, in so far as I have a plan, for the rest of the book is to supplement some of the incomplete information contained in *Many Mansions* by knowledge which has come to me since I finished writing it, and to make sure that I shall not be reproached for leaving unsubstantiated any statement made in Chapter IV of this book.

If I can do that, and finish up with a chapter on Religion as affected by revelation, I shall have covered my subject. Some of the remaining chapters, however, may, from the nature of what I have to say, appear to be a little disconnected.

I think that I will now give you the story of James. It came through in four instalments, and I feel sure that it was intended for publication, or else we should not have been asked to devote so much of our time to it.

Notice how he is constantly making fresh discoveries and finding that his discoveries have often been only illusions after all.

We too must keep an open mind, and we must not be discouraged in our search for Truth even though our most cherished idols are demolished in the process.

That puzzling phrase 'Except ye become as little children…' means, I think, that we must retain, not the child's unlimited credulity, but the child's openness to receive impressions, and that we must give them a fair examination uninhibited by preconceived ideas.

(It also means, of course, that we must return to the child's attitude of trustfulness, knowing that its needs will be provided for by those to whom it looks for the necessities of life.) Well, here is the story of James.

19/10/43.

"They have told me to talk and tell you what has been happening. I never thought that I would use you as a secretary. I won't go back to my actual passing yet, I will tell you about my work.

(He is showing planes going out in V formation with himself in front.) "I led them and am still leading them. Flying was my life. When I woke up over here, and realised that it was over for me, it didn't seem worthwhile going on.

"I didn't realise at first that I had got mine. I woke up in a hospital, a bright airy place with about six beds in the room. It was the nicest hospital I had ever seen. Great French windows wide open, and it was built practically right on the sands. I love the sea, and I lay and watched the changing colours and the seagulls for a long time. I had a charming nurse who seemed to be always there at the right moment. I had leg and chest wounds. One day I realised that although the dressings were regularly done I had had no pain, there didn't seem to be any blood on the bandages or any sign that I really needed them. I began to wriggle my leg; it felt fine. I thumped my chest; that was all right too. So next time my nurse came along I tackled her, and suddenly realised that I had not seen a doctor. The nurse laughed and said she would show me a bit of sleight of hand. She put her hand on my chest and said ' Hey presto, disappear!' and when I felt, the bandages were gone. She did the same with my leg, and told me I had been quite cured for a long time, but I wouldn't face up to it. I felt a bit annoyed. I hadn't thought of myself as a malingerer, so I just hopped out of bed, and told her to bring my clothes damn quick. She just laughed, and said ' Look at yourself.' And suddenly there was a mirror on the wall; it might have been there, but I hadn't noticed it there before. I looked in it and lo and behold I was fully dressed.

"This fairly bowled me over. I've seen some magicians in my time, but this was the finest performance I'd ever seen. I even had my disc on my wrist, and I had particularly noticed that I wasn't wearing it in bed. It had rather bothered me, that, in case I should have difficulty in getting out again.

"I was rather puzzled, and had a nasty feeling at the pit of my stomach. Somehow I was beginning to know; but I wouldn't stop to think. I asked the nurse to explain things. She took my hand in hers and just looked at me. I knew then. But somehow I grew warm again. Well, I suppose I might as well tell you. I howled on her shoulder like a kid. It did me good. Then she took me outside onto a terrace and we looked over the sea; the horizon was dull and very misty. I could see what I took to be planes flying very low. She told me that that was the borderland and that they really were planes, that the R.A.F. still functioned, and that I could join them if I wanted to. That put new heart into me, to feel that I could still carry on, but she wouldn't let me go, and turned me round so that I was looking inland. The fields and the meadows, the rivers, and away in the distance a misty range, and everything so beautifully bright, and she told me I could go on. We did go for a little while into the fields. It was peaceful. We talked about things and she explained to me that I was on the edge of a great and wonderful country and there was no need for me to go back, I had paid the price. But I didn't look at it that way. The job just wasn't finished. So I said the country could wait, if this is eternity there's lots of time.

"She laughed and took my hand and said, 'Well, if that's how you feel about it, you had better come and meet the others.'

"I met the others at the Base. There's a big hall there, and you enlist just as you do down below. It's all very orderly, but I won't describe that tonight. I enlisted in Fighter Command, among the boys. And I have made another friend, a friendship I hope to have time to cultivate when the job is done. There are lots of us here who thank our nurse for helping us over the difficult time of realisation.

"I'll tell you more next time we meet. I'll be in the vanguard. I'll tell you about meeting my brother sometime."

James (2) 26/10/43.

"Good evening Sir. I think I told you about my waking up. I will try to describe our headquarters; it will take some doing.

"The headquarters; to which I am attached is situated in a valley surrounded by hills. We have operations rooms and the whole business is there; you know, you might just say that it is a complete replica of the headquarters of any flying unit anywhere.

"There is a large hall where we have musters, and the boys entertain themselves, and here we have the notice-board where we .put up the names of those about whom we wish to have some information.

"We have a reading room as well, with very fine books and magazines; it is the finest reading room I have ever known, you positively cannot ask for any book, paper or magazine which is not here. I have a sneaking feeling myself that some of them, indeed a lot of them, aren't really here until they are asked for.

"There is a canteen too; some of the boys still feel in need of food and drink, but more and more of them are learning to feed themselves, and by 'feed' I mean refresh themselves from the atmosphere.

"You will be surprised to know that the runways are situated on the mountain tops and not in the valley; quite a reversal, isn't it? You see the planes we fly, although constructed in the same way as those our comrade's fly on earth, are made of very different materials. Every plane that a man ever flew has been rebuilt over here, but now they are indestructible.

"To get back to the runways—we start off along our strips which are not of concrete but electrical vibrations (moving streams of light). We take off up above so that we don't have to rise. That is a general view.

"Now I will tell you about my first flight. We work in squadrons still, but each man knows that he has to attach himself to one of our heavy planes. We are all fighters over here, Interceptors. We have no bombers. I went out from my mountaintop, and I can't tell you how good it was to feel the stick once more. You see it's a solid stick to me

94

because we are both made of the same type of matter, though I hate to think what your reactions would be; it would feel like a silk thread to you. (But I fly every night.) Don't I know it? Don't I fly with you? But I am talking of you as you are now.

"It's rather different flying here because you are no longer responsible for the squadron, you know that nothing can happen to them now; and so you can give your whole attention to the one plane to which you have attached yourself.

"I set off, and for a little while I was only conscious of the great joy of being in it once again. Then I realised that the job was still going on. I thought of the plane I wished to be with, and suddenly I went down into the mists. They overcame me for a little while, I was flying blind. I could see nothing but the fog. I got a bit panicky—funny how the weather still gets you. You remember Sir, it was always the weather and never Jerry that bothered us. I was wondering just what use I could be if the fog didn't clear, when I suddenly heard someone speak. It seemed to come over the intercom. 'Why don't you fix your mind on the target? You won't get out of the mist until you decide where you're going.' I thought this was a bit thick. After all I had received no instructions, so I yelled back' where is the blooming target?' " 'There's half a dozen to choose from,' I was told. 'Where would you like to go?' I rubbed my hands. 'Oh boy, oh boy, choose your target! Berlin is mine.' In an instant I was back in the thick of it. I was flying inside a bomber, yes, plane and all. I could hear in a strange way what was being said. I don't quite understand how I picked it up, but I believe that we can tune in to the wavelength of w/t just as you can. Anyhow I heard quite distinctly this conversation:

"'Two minutes and we shall be over the target.'

"'Good, we'll let them have merry hell.'

"I didn't listen to any more because I suddenly realised I should be outside the plane. The silly asses were far too low. When they came over the target they were right in the line of the explosion from the bombs of the previous planes. It was my task to try to divert the repercussions so that they could get away in time. They did, but I felt annoyed because they should have known better than to take such risks. I went after them to give them a hearty telling off, forgetting they couldn't hear me anyhow. They were so pleased with themselves; they hadn't a thought of danger. Then I saw it was no use; they'd do it the next time anyway, but I couldn't resist trying. I don't know just how I managed it, but I put all my will into the thought, and I said over the intercom to that pilot 'You fool, we might have been blown to blazes, why did you fly so low?' He heard me. I won't tell you what he said back. It really was quite fun to hear them telling each other to mind their own business. I can't tell you what it meant just to be in it again; I felt I was one of them, and though they would never know who was monkeying with them that night, I'll never forget it. I've given up trying to teach them sense, they haven't got anywhere their own safety is concerned. I think it was an Irishman who was bomb aimer, because of the feeling of the words that came to me when 'bombs gone' came over. There were three fighter attacks before they made base. The strange thing was the way the bullets went right through me, but when they did this I could direct them. I couldn't direct them until they were within me. So some of them hit the plane of course because, fast as I can move, I couldn't draw all the fire. It was only the undercarriage that was damaged that trip. They made a good landing. I heard one of them say 'Jolly good trip! Puts life into a fellow, that does.' He didn't know how much life it had put into a dead airman to be able to come back and carry on.

"I'm not one who can talk easily about things which mean a great deal to me but, as I stood there, close to the tarmac, seeing it all through a haze, the familiar things—feeling the familiar sounds, I knew without any shadow of doubt that God is, and that He is good." (Do I know your nurse?) " Yes you've guessed." (His nurse was my wife.)

James (3).

Now I want to tell you how I became aware of the fact that all that was really past" for me.

"My helper was explaining to me that our headquarters and our operations room and our planes are all imaginary and unnecessary. They are built very close to the earth only because we men feel the need of them, in what I shall term the first waking hours over here.

"I will tell you how it happened. We stood together on a mountainside looking over a clear runway. It was a perfect taking-off field, quite empty. My helper, whom I shall call Miziah, asked me what plane I wanted to send out now. I thought of a Spitfire, and lo and behold there was a Spitfire ready to take off, with the engine turning over. Then Miziah suggested to me in some subtle way that perhaps another type of plane would be better. I thought of a Beaufighter, and that was there; the Spitfire had gone.

"I did this once or twice and realised that they are but the stuff that dreams are made of. Until now I had walked about everywhere, with the single exception of wishing myself in the fight. I had even climbed this mountain side (and quite enjoyed it too). Miziah asked me if I would like to get down quickly and where I would like to be. I suddenly thought of a quiet seashore and I was there. I can't explain to you what that did to me. It was a terrific shock, and the first inkling I had that the laws governing the physical world no longer applied to me.

"We rested awhile by the sea. I'd like to tell you about this seashore. The water is like the earth water, never at peace, always moving; and yet there is no sense of restlessness with it such as one sometimes feels on earth. I bathed in it. It revitalised me. I couldn't sink in it, and it isn't wet. I said to Miziah 'I believe I could walk on the water,' and before I'd finished speaking I was walking on it. That water purifies the soul. In it one loses all weariness of spirit, all sadness and sorrow, and gains peace. We often bathe there.

"I thought of my brother, and Miziah told me I could go and see him now. I found him in a home of rest. He had taken badly to his new life, and refused to face the fact, and just as some people on earth retire to bed with an illness of the body, which is brought about by their lack of stamina to face the difficulties of their everyday life, so he was suffering from an illness of the etheric body, brought about by his fear of facing what had happened.

"I was able to help him, because at first he thought he was back on the earth with me, and that what he had been thinking about was imaginary. You see he was young, just a boy, and had so much to live for, but when he realised that I had stopped mine too, he faced up to things, and left the home of rest quite prepared for anything which might come. Miziah explained to me that he had been suffering from severe shock, and that my familiar face had just done the trick. So you see, in spite of everything, my demise wasn't quite useless.

"My brother wasn't unhappy; he just wanted something familiar, he did think a lot of me and was not so good at adjusting himself, but he's fine now. Give my love to my mother and to all of them."

James (4).

"I never really understood what eternity meant before. I don't know if I shall be able to convey to you the glory and magnitude of it all. Words are so inadequate, but I'll try.

"The elder brother introduced me to a friend in the group who was to show me where I might live if I wished. Remember at this time I was still in the mists. Miziah told me to clothe myself ready for the journey and gave me what might be termed an asbestos cloak. We didn't walk or float, we just moved. Gradually the mists were left behind and we were in a belt of blinding light. This was why I required the asbestos cloak because I had not yet made my decision as to whether I should leave the mists. Miziah had no need of a cloak. On the other side of this belt is a land more beautiful than any words can describe. I found myself at a little cottage where I left my cloak. A very beautiful young woman owned the cottage and showed, me her garden filled with the most beautiful flowers. Then we went down a little path to the beach, Miziah told me to bathe. You talk about the Mediterranean blue; the blue of the Mediterranean is muddy compared to this. I bathed and found I could swim under water without the slightest inconvenience.

I could see sea anemones, pebbles and fishes. I seemed to stay in the waiter quite a time. It buoyed me up; I felt marvellous, and when I came but of the sea I felt clean, cleanliness such as I have never experienced before. Then we set off through the woods where the very trees are alive and a part of one. The grass caresses one's feet in these woods; the bird song has to be heard to be believed.

"We came out of the woods and passed through a little village. It was rather like an Alpine village. The people all came to the doors of the cottages to wave and smile at us. I thought they were greeting Miziah, and they were; but he said they came to the gates for me, to show me how glad they were that I was coming home.

"We climbed a hill out of the village and had a magnificent view of the surrounding country. The little range of hills we were in stretched out and up to a great plateau and away in the distance were mighty mountains; those mountains are the beginning of another world, Miziah told me.

"Close on the hillside was a little house like a hunting-lodge. As we looked at this little house, suddenly we were there, standing on the veranda. What a mighty view! The hillside, the village, the woods, the sea, and the great mountains and plateau to rest one's eyes. The peace was past understanding, and this, Miziah told me, was my home. I could stay here, work with my friends in the village, and receive visitors from beyond the plateau. I was to make my choice. I made it. I couldn't desert the boys. Perhaps I could help them through the belt of light. Help them to realise that they might retire honourably from the Service and cross into this haven themselves. It is too good a place to keep hidden for one's own use.

"Miziah told me he had expected this would be my answer; that was why I required the asbestos cloak, so that I could return as I am and be with the boys, not as a leader or messenger as he is, but just one of themselves, so that they'd listen to me and put away the illusions they hold so dearly.

"Before we returned to the cottage Miziah took me within the fold of his cloak and took me beyond the plateau, that I might see even dimly in the distance some of the real Heaven-world. I cannot describe what I saw or the glory of the experience when a great ray of light shone out and encompassed me. I only know that in that moment I realised with a realisation that can never fade that the Master knows us each and every one.

"That's inadequate Sir, but it's the best I can do.

"That little village is on the outer edge of the heaven-spheres where reality begins, and the illusions of self, of separateness, of greatness, fall away. They are consumed in that belt of light, but having passed through it in the natural course of events, it takes a long time to re-establish contact with the mists. I have no time to lose. When the job is finished we'll go through it, all of us, gladly and let you folks get on with it, while we are learning to fit ourselves for the next job.

"Signing off now."

Here I think I should like to refer to a criticism which has reached me indirectly from several sources. People have said "I can't understand how Lord Dowding can tell us that, after all their sacrifice, our boys are given nothing better to do than to go on fighting against the Germans." I feel that I must have been to blame to have given this impression, which is substantially untrue, although it is certainly true that men killed in the heat of battle often go on fighting (or trying to fight) because they don't know that anything has happened to them.

Also in the earliest stages of the new life the instinct to continue the war against the enemy does persist for a little while in some cases. A lad called Teddy (one of the supporters of the boy who was our first 'Rescue' case), told me that he was the leader of the 'Squadron of Retaliation.' "Not being vindictive (he explained) just evening up the score."

I expect he soon learned to think differently; anyway I never heard any more about his Squadron and its doings.

No, the work of those who stay voluntarily in the region of the Earth mists is mainly that of meeting their comrades and helping them across the border.

Of those who participate more actively in battle, we have just had an example in James, though even that phase did not last very long with him.

Peter was another. Peter has thrown himself heart and soul into the work of protecting air crews. His attitude is that there are plenty to deal with those who come over. He is working day and night to protect those still on the job. He says: — "

I fly with the Bomber crews. Here is a strange fact—when the bombs are released, I have quickly to remove myself from the machine. The explosion does something to us over here. I keep intending to investigate this, but somehow I haven't got down to it yet. All I know is that (strange thing) it can still knock us out. So that, while the bombs are going down and exploding, we have to leave the lads alone—alone, so far as we lower-grade people are concerned. Then, once over the target and away, we can pick up again. Machine guns have no effect whatever on us.

"I have a special plane. I won't give you particulars, but I can tell you that the mascot is a black 'Felix the Cat' painted on."

(I was telling this story at one of my meetings, and at this point one of the lads in the invisible audience began to jump up and down with excitement, and said: —

"That's *my* mascot, he's talking about me!" His pal turned to him and said, "shut up you ass, you 're dead.")

Peter continues:

"Teddy and Derek are members of the crew. Fine lads! It won't be my fault if they don't come back safely each time.

"A call has come, I must go; I will come again." I hope I have said enough to indicate that, except during the first stages of readjustment to the new life, any 'fighting' that they do is entirely protective and not aggressive.

Now I expect that readers of *Many Mansions* would like to see some more of the messages from people brought by Colonel Gascoigne and transmitted through his daughter, Mrs. Hill. Out of a large number I choose the four which follow.

The first is from a Gunner Subaltern. He doesn't say where he was killed, but I think it was in Italy.

"It is very good of your father to let me write through you; yes, we do a lot of work together, I am very glad to help.

"I was a gunner, and much older than most of the men whom I was commanding, but that didn't seem to matter when we received a direct hit and were all bowled out. I could gather my wits together quicker than they could, and I saw your father and brought him into our Mess, and I tell you it was a mess . . . though we'd got away from our bodies no one really knew what had happened; some of them were beginning to see, others were catching snatches of music in between horrible memories of the actual fighting. I think now it must have felt like a madhouse coming into our circle, but your father wasn't in the least surprised.

"I got a lot into a little pocket behind a knoll from which they couldn't see their bodies; I was scared that they'd get out and see all the refuse of our camp, but luckily they hadn't got the hang of walking, so that didn't happen.

"It's queer how the habit of thinking of someone else helps one in a crisis like this; I don't remember thinking about myself at all; I just wasn't there so as to matter, but I saw and heard and felt everything. I saw the men as my children; it was my job to guard and help them. They were all at sixes and sevens, some seemed to be going through awful nightmares; others were asleep, dead asleep, from which we couldn't rouse them, others were in a sort of coma, very drowsy. I grasped it all quite suddenly and called for aid. It had become a habit of mine, and I felt confident that someone would turn up, and very soon I saw Harris, the Captain who had been our adjutant and had been killed three days earlier.

I saw him and tried to reach him, but my feet! Well, they wouldn't work; I could go up and down, but not along the ground, it was too maddening, I felt like Alice in Wonderland! I laughed and yelled to him and he heard and saw me floundering about in the air, like a daddy longlegs as he described it. 'Oh, you, is it,' he said. 'I thought I'd know your clumsy feet. Treading on air are you? Well how d'you like it?' This fairly sobered me, and I liked him better for that downright welcome and chaff than for any amount of sympathy. 'Oh,' I said, trying to look as though it were all quite natural, 'Can you give me a line on this joint, I haven't done a course on the death penalty!' We talked on like that; I was hysterical, but it helped me, and made it all seem more natural.

He came down to where I was; he saw my people scattered about and spotted my batman Jones; he wasn't much of a soldier (Jones); delicate sort of fellow, not a heavy sleeper at any time, arid now he was waking up and looking for all the world like a shocked dormouse. I think he was hurt and disappointed at not being met by at least an Apostle, and seemed incline' to doze off again, but Harris stirred him up and called him to help with the others. Jones just couldn't face life at first, he was distressed at leaving his body and wanted to go and find it, and he couldn't think why our Lord hadn't met him. I didn't think about it, I knew it was a futile thought; who were we to be met by the Lord of Heaven? Anyhow we weren't properly dead; at least that's how it seemed to me.

"Harris joked and scolded and got him at last to forget himself and we tried to wake a few of the others, but it WAS such hard work, I felt utterly exhausted; at last Harris put his hand on my shoulder and said, 'James, old man, you've done your spot, come and rest,' and he brought me to your father. ..."

(Next day) "Yes please may I finish? Well, I met your father in real earnest; you see he had been there all the time, but he couldn't help us much at that stage, excepting by standing close, and wishing us power.

"Soon, when the weariness had left us, I saw the living force which I was drawing from him, and I lived again in the Power that he gave me. It was all new to me; it was like eating, drinking, rest and exercise all in one. I felt and knew that I was near a dynamo, I was transformed. I was happy and confident and knew that all would be well.

"He took me with him; I don't know how we went, but we arrived and I saw many others who'd reached my state of awareness.

We were by the sea in a lovely place, but I wasn't happy, I wanted to go back to my men, but your father said ' No . . . not until you have learnt to use your mind, and send out rays of healing and life, you will not be any good.'

"So I went to school again. The Captain was there, too; he had done quite a bit so he could help me. It was confusing but very interesting.

"We were told to look upon our minds as tanks of living fluid which we could vaporise, and throw upon the ether in any direction that we wished and according to the type of help required. The power varied in each of us. Doctors had more healing power and were able to direct it more accurately. Artists were able to surround the sufferer with beauty that was more easily absorbed; musicians produced the sound vibrations, and so on, but in the main our powers were not so varied as our capacity to direct them.

"I am still at work on this, but I have begun to work with the men and your father is my C.O. It's A1 to have someone like him. I can't tell you what he has done for me, and how much I love and admire him. Just let me tell you my name is Jack, and I love the work over here."

The next is from a munitions worker called Bill Edwards.

"Oh how badly I want to write home and tell them it's all blather, this fuss about death. Can't you help me? I'm as much alive as I ever was, but I know, if you write, it wouldn't make any difference because they don't know you, and they'd just think you mad.

What CAN I do . . .? Ah, yes, I see, I'm to ask your father did you say? Who's he? The man beside me now? Why, he can't be your father, he's half your age! Well, he's a nice young fellow anyway. Thanks for the tip. I'll tell you how we get on. Thank you.

EDWARDS."

"Yes, thank you, it was dark down there you know, and suffocating. No, I'm not a soldier, only a munitions maker. I was done in in the last London raid. I was underground, and the floor gave way, and all the machinery on top came down onto us; it was an awful show, I screamed when I saw it coming. The fire broke out before anyone could stop it, and I saw it coming towards me—fire and tangled parts of machinery and molten metal; there wasn't a chance of escaping for any of us. The pain didn't last very long, but much longer than our bodies. I kept on feeling it whenever I looked at my body, and I couldn't leave it somehow until Jane came. Jane is a girl who worked near me; she came and took my arm and led me away.

"Jane is a riddle; I knew it was Jane, but I'd never seen her really before, and suddenly I saw that she was LOVELY; her eyes and hair, and everything about her. I couldn't think why I hadn't been crazy about her all along, but she was just Jane to me, like a lot of others, dirty and tired and covered with oil-stained clothes. I said, 'Jane, but you're beautiful, and I love you,' and she just looked at me and laughed and said, 'Oh, Bill, ain't you soft. I've loved you always, but you had to be dead before you got some sense.'

"'Dead,' I ses. 'Dead, wot the hell d'you mean? No, I'm not dead,' and then seeing I was getting all worked up, she soothed me like a child and told me not to worry. 'Well, I'm here, aren't I, Bill? And I aren't dead neither, so be a good boy and stop worrying.' I did, and I followed her in a sort of sleepy way, I felt heavier and heavier until I slept good and proper, and when I woke up I wasn't feeling nearly so strange and Jane was sitting on the grass nearby playing with two kiddies. I called to her and she brought them over to me. 'Look, Bill,' she ses, 'these are our kids' 'Our kids,' I ses, 'not on your honour, I ain't got no kids by nobody,' and she laughs and ses, 'That's all over now, Bill, and I mean we've got to look after them . . . They was ours in some place long, long ago, least that's wot they told me; you see, Bill, we've lived through death, p'raps we've lived before we were born like, I don't know, but it don't seem as though we'd ever not been, if you can follow me. You and me, Bill, have got to scratch along together like, as we did on earth. But this is lovely, and we don't work any more.' "I can't go on now, may I come again?

JANE AND BILL."

The third is from an Irish soldier.

"I see what I'm to do. It's kind of easy once you've given me the chance, but oh, dear me, there are barriers and all kinds of difficulties. I didn't want to force my way home with so much feeling this way and that, but when I'd 'bought' it I found there was nothing much to do (I never liked foreign parts) old Ireland for me every time, and tho' I didn't want to go home because of the domestic troubles, the call of Home was too strong and I found I was There, and all the family grieving for me as tho' I'd been a hero, beloved of them all! Sure, I could have held my sides for laughing, and me, large as life, and still there, but all invisible; it seemed queer too, and just the opportunity to pay off old scores against them who'd hurt me in the young days. I'd come close to them at dusk and shout thoughts into their brains. First, I tried just shouting, but they couldn't hear, so that was no good. Then I learnt to think the thoughts into their brains, the same as I'm doing with you. I made them remember me, and fear me, and think that I was haunting them, and would continue to do so unless they were kind to those I loved. That worked very well and I was enjoying it until I came across the Colonel, my old battalion commander, and he ses to me, 'Why do you do this, Murphy? Don't you see you're wasting your time? You mustn't use the power of hate to protect love any more than we use poison gas to protect our cities. You must use Love for Love, but only Love, and you'll succeed.'

" 'What,' ses J, 'Go love spinning for the priest? No,' ses I, 'Sure I can't feel love for him, and the likes of him.'

" 'Well, have it your own way,' ses the Colonel, 'but you'll only hurt yourself if you do anything else; he is in the earth body, and you can't hurt him near as much as he can hurt you with hate thoughts in your ether body. It's like pitting a man in a bathing dress against one in full flying kit; anyway, Murphy, there's more work that's worthwhile to be done, and your work too.' So I went with him for a time until I was called home by thoughts so insistent that I had to go.

"It was wee Mary, our youngest, only two years old; and she got sick with the pneumonia, and the wife prayed and prayed, but it didn't do any good. I sat by her side, the wee one, she was so bad, I could feel her little hand all hot and feverish; and then suddenly she looked up and saw me, and climbed out of her cot into my arms, just like she used to do, and I held her forever so long in great happiness; and then I thought maybe I'd best put her into her cot again, and as I went to do it I saw she was in bed lying so quiet and still, and a child just like her was in my arms; and as I turned, uncertain what to do, a beautiful lady came and said to me 'Take her with you, no need to stay in the house now, take her into the sunshine, she is yours now and for always, and she will be your special care.'

"So I took her out and we sat on the hillside, and played with flowers and pebbles, and when I'd left her asleep out there I went back into the house, I found only grief and mourning . . . and then I knew that wee Mary had come to join me . . . and I understood that death wasn't real, but Life everlasting was TRUE, TRUE, TRUE. ..."

And lastly there is a little Christmas message from Colonel Gascoigne himself.

"Now that the shops are empty, you say there is nothing to give, but do GIVE something all the same.

"The gift is all-important, not for its own intrinsic value, but as a symbol of Goodwill.

"To each friend you send something of your substance of earth, something of your substance of Spirit; it is a Sacrament between you.

"Giving and receiving are the Sacraments of human Love, just as you give and receive from God in the Communion Service.

"Bless each gift as you send it forth with all your Goodwill, so that it may enhance the beauty and relieve the pain of Life, for that one who receives.

"And you, when you receive, open your mind, not only to the gift, but to the Spirit of Love, Sacrifice and Thought that has been spent upon its creation.

"So ... if you exchange only pebbles at your Christmas Feast, the Love reaped through them need not be less than in the rich careless days of the past."

I will finish this chapter with a story from Z which came to me in the following way.

"During the summer of 1944 L.L. had to take a prolonged rest from her work, and I found myself running more and more short of fresh material for the meetings which I addressed. I always tried to have something fresh for each meeting when possible, so I sent out a S.O.S. and the story of Antony came to me from the North of Scotland. Here it is:

30/8/44.

"Greetings to my brother. I bring the story of one who overcame his own lower self and in helping others purified and raised his own soul.

"Truly love is the key of the universe; with it all things are possible; without it nothing is possible.

"Antony was born in a small village in Eastern Europe. He was the eldest of three boys. A poor peasant family, the parents yet had a high standard of morality.

"The mother was old before her time from hard work and the necessity of feeding and clothing her family with very little money. The father was a sturdy man, honest and hard working. He cultivated the little patch of ground round his house and also earned a little by woodcutting in the forest.

"Antony was a bright-eyed boy of sixteen, already taking much of the work from his father's shoulders and caring for his youngest brother who had been born a cripple and could not walk from birth!

"The day the enemy came into that little village Antony was in the woods with his brother. The cripple lay on a bed of moss Antony had selected, and while the elder boy chopped and stacked, the younger sang the songs they both loved in a clear treble. Antony could not sing and it was a joke between them when he would shout out a chorus.

"They did not hear the enemy coming and were surprised and unafraid when the soldiers came through the trees.

"Then followed an unforgettable scene for Antony. Finding the cripple boy the soldiers killed him with the bayonet and his cries tore Antony's heart to shreds. But he was helpless. Two soldiers held him and when he struggled, one twisted and broke his right arm, so he was helpless. In pain of body and agony of spirit he was marched back to the village where he found his mother and father and many others lined up before a wall. Antony broke loose and ran to them but he did not reach them. A bullet sent him quickly after his crippled brother. But he went into the astral world filled with hatred and fear and pain, and he built around himself a belt of desolation which none could penetrate. He wandered in the dim light ever seeking those who had hurt his brother and gradually there grew round him a band of others who also hated, and they sent out strong wave-lengths of hate and revenge to feed those on the earth who live on such things.

"But the cripple boy loved Antony with a deep and abiding love and he tried over and over again to penetrate the darkness and the malicious forms surrounding him.

"Now Antony did not love evil, though evil had him temporarily in its grip. So came the time when Antony found himself again in the forest and there lay one of the enemy wounded. Antony was not aware that there was any difference between their states. He only knew here was the hated enemy at his mercy.

"Stealthily he crept up to the moaning man and sat gloating over his pain, while he wondered how he could make him suffer more.

As he sat there the man's pain grew worse for his aura became impregnated with Antony's malignant thoughts.

"Then a strange thing happened. Antony heard his brother singing the verse of ah old song. His heart grew hot with longing, his eyes filled with tears. But the hate in his heart grew stronger and the song died away.

"Then Antony became aware that men were in the forest searching and he went near to them then and turned them from the path which led to the wounded man. Back again he stood and looked at the soldier. He was young and not unlike Antony's second brother. Antony felt a moment's compassion and bent over the pain-wracked mail.

"Again came the sound of his brother singing, and again the flood of rage and fear swept over Antony, but he did not lose sight of the man on the ground.

"Reluctantly Antony rose; against the urging of hate and revenge rose the teaching of his parents, the memory of the kindness of his brother to every maimed animal and bird.

"Slowly Antony went back to the searchers. After some time he came close to one of them and said, 'Go to the left—go to the left.' The soldier did not hear, but he paused and looked around.

Again and again Antony spoke and at last the soldier turned down the path. Antony followed him and saw him reach the wounded man.

"Antony felt suddenly glad, light of heart, and he heard his brother calling. He ran through the wood out of the dim darkness into the daylight to meet his brother, no longer a cripple.

"The sight of his brother in a straight and healthy body filled Antony with joy and awe and he realised what had happened to them both.

"His brother's love had helped him in his darkest need and the love of the One who had commanded him to do what He had risen to do— To return good for evil.

"That love of Angel and of man combined overcometh all things. Call upon it my friends, it is ever available."

CHAPTER XI

MEDIUMS AND PSYCHICS

Now perhaps it might interest you to hear some of my experiences with mediums outside our own circle.

I should explain that I do not join any other circle and I do not sit with other mediums except for some good and sufficient reason. It has been indicated to me that it is desirable to avoid any unnecessary mixing of vibrations.

The most common reason for the breaking of my rule is the information that there is a group of R.A.F. boys on the other side who would appreciate a visit. In such cases I always try to go at once, to talk with them and to wish them well.

One such visit I paid at the kind invitation of Mrs. Estelle Roberts. At the sitting the Direct Voice was employed, with a spirit named Red Cloud in charge of the proceedings.

The séance was ably reported in the *Psychic News* of October 23rd, 1943, and I will not occupy space by any detailed account of the events.

It will suffice to say that 16 people were present in addition to the invisible visitors, and I think I am right in saying that every one of us received at least one verbal message. The "boys" behaved in a very light-hearted way, contending for possession of the 'trumpet' and indulging in an impromptu competition as to who could raise it highest into the air. Mrs. Roberts gave her services gratuitously and, when offerings were thrust upon her, she handed the whole amount to me to be given to the R.A.F. Benevolent Fund.

I mention the name of Mrs. Estelle Roberts gratefully and freely because the proceedings have already been reported in the press. If I am
less forthcoming with other names and addresses, it is not from any
lack of appreciation and gratitude, but because, in these days of spas-
modic and arbitrary persecution of mediums, publicity of this nature
might bring harm where nothing but gratitude is intended.

At 'another place,' then, I attended by invitation to see the working
of an instrument known as the 'Communigraph.' This is a table with
a ground-glass top and with a pendulum hanging underneath. The
pendulum hangs over a circular alphabet and can be moved round so
as to hang over any letter. If it is then pressed down, the corresponding letter is lit up under the ground glass and remains illuminated until the pendulum is released. (A photograph of the apparatus appears
on page 30 of a book named *A New Conception of Love* by Sir Vincent
Caillard. Rider & Co.)

The first thing that happened was an uncanny rattling of the apparatus beneath the table, and then the word CASWALL was spelt out. This
puzzled everyone except myself, for it is my second name. I said, "Yes.
That is my name," and the answer came "You were named after me."

Caswall was the name of my paternal grandmother, so the visitor
must have been my great-grandfather at least. However, he made but a
short stay because he had come to introduce Colonel Gascoigne, who
wanted to see how the instrument worked before he tried it himself.

I told him that I had just had a letter from a psychic paper asking me
if I was sure that he was alive. He replied, "Yes, yes, yes, of course I am
alive, dammit," somewhat to the scandal of the owners of the instrument,
who explained that it, had never used language like that before.

There was one other amusing feature of the instrument, and that
was a number of gramophone records piled up in the centre of the circular alphabet. I asked what that was for, and was told, "Oh, that's to
make the spirits use the pendulum properly. It is made to swing "round
over the circle of letters, but they don't understand this and are always
breaking the mechanism by pulling it straight across the circle." The
apparatus seemed to be rather slow and clumsy in operation, and "after 20 minutes or so, we switched to the Direct Voice, which was not
produced by a trumpet but by an arrangement like two opened toy umbrellas opposite one another and swinging round a central pivot.

The voices produced by this machine seemed to be much less hoarse
and more lifelike than those produced by the trumpet. Lady Caillard's
voice in particular was marvellously clear and sweet.

All this time we were in pitch-darkness, and luckily I had been warned not to be alarmed if I felt some sort of physical contact.

Even so, however, I got a bit of a shock when I received half a dozen firm pats on the head from the Colonel.

Now please remember that I am not telling you this as 'Proof of Survival.' We did not tie the medium in her chair with sealed ropes nor take flashlight photographs at unexpected moments. We went by invitation to talk to our friends by a new method, and I, for one, was profoundly grateful for the opportunity. I accept proof of survival not from materialisations and signs and wonders, but from the mental contacts, which I make with my friends and acquaintances and dear ones on the other side. I am completely and absolutely certain that the operators of the apparatus were not cheating, and I believe that they could not have done so, but I am not going to argue the point.

What I have to say is that at this place I was present when three apports were materialised. A tiny silver crucifix with the word Jerusalem on the back, a larger hollow silver cross with a leaf pattern, and a little gold ring with ivy leaves and the inscription 'I cling to thee.' Two of these were put into my hands.

The happenings at this place were too intimate and personal for inclusion in this book, but on one visit I made four physical contacts. The first a vigorous handshake from Colonel Gascoigne, and the second with my dear wife. The third came from an airman who was grateful to me for the altogether minor part, which I had played in helping him to make contact with his wife and mother. He showed his gratitude by picking the 'umbrellas' off their pivot and tapping me on the head with them, much to the mental agony of the owners, who feared that he would break them. But he replaced them on their pivot gently and without hesitation.

The fourth contact came from the Negro child who has attached herself especially to this apparatus. Hers is usually the first voice which comes through. She rather likes being teased in a good humoured way, and I was pretending to believe that she could not see in the dark. She said "I can see your nose," and I received a vigorous pinch on that organ.

At yet another place I saw full materialisations in a red light. These phenomena have been so often described that I shall not include a long account of the séance. There are just three things which I shall mention about this sitting.

The first is that though we did not see the figures build up behind the simple curtain which was the only cabinet, we saw them as it were sink into a loose heap on the floor when they went, and they frequently held open the curtain so that the medium and the materialised form were seen simultaneously.

The second is that one of the figures passed across my front to the person sitting on my right, and the drapery of her robe fell across my knee. I picked it up gently in my hand. It was like very fine mosquito netting, very soft and limp, very dry, and with an extraordinary feeling of perfect cleanness, if you can understand what I mean.

The third was a visitor who came to me. Most of the forms remained within a few feet of the curtain, but this woman walked out into the middle of the room and picked up a small table on which were lying pencil and paper. She carried the table back and set it down immediately in front of me. I felt in my pocket and asked "Have you got a pencil?" but she tapped on the table to show that she had already picked up the pencil which was lying there. She then wrote her name 'July' on two separate bits of paper, and went back behind the curtain.

Clarice said afterwards "She is a very beautiful and dear friend from our side. July. It was clever of her to move the table, she has done it before."

To tell you the honest truth, I don't much like materialisations of the human form. One knows that what one sees or feels is not they, but a borrowed envelope built up for the occasion.

They are so real to me without this artifice that the synthetic form detracts from, rather than increases, their reality.

But this is only a personal idiosyncrasy, and others, I know, derive a deep satisfaction from the sight and touch of their loved ones. There is also their point of view to be, considered, and there are many on the other side who, in spite of the great effort involved, are made very happy by being able to recapture, even for a minute, the physical sensations which they left behind with their Earth bodies.

Then there are several home circles which I have visited from time to time, generally because they have made contact with some little R.A.F. coterie and are doing the same sort of work as we are in our circle. My own idea is that these 'Lighthouses' are likely to increase considerably in numbers during the next few years, and that it is through them, rather than through large organised bodies, that the true Light will spread among the people at large. In any case, I am sure that their work is very important.

Let me give an instance of the sort of thing which happens on these occasions.

The lady in question was accustomed to work in trance.

First Vale Owen spoke through her and gave an idea of the vast armies of earthbound spirits who are awaiting an awakening through an earth-link and of the desperate need for mediums who will selflessly dedicate themselves to this work.

Then my wife came through and to establish her identity told me something I had done for her soon after she died which no other soul on earth ever knew anything about.

Then came a sailor boy to be woken up. He was very cold and wretched. He had died of exposure on a raft.

Then my new friend began to whistle tunelessly. I couldn't make out for a time what she was trying to render, but at last I guessed 'Here's a health unto his Majesty.'

It turned out to be a sailor, the leader of a group of seven. They had been torpedoed in an ammunition ship from which very few had been saved.

I asked him what they were doing and he said "Oh, just jigging along with a mouth organ."

"That isn't going to help you much. Why don't you try to get somewhere?"

"We're waiting for the fog to lift. If you were a sailor you'd know that you can't get anywhere in an Atlantic fog; you just have to wait for it to lift."

"Well, how did you get here? This isn't the Atlantic."

"Oh we saw a man with a Cross and we followed him." (Sheepishly.)

"I've never had much to do with a Cross before."

"Well, perhaps you will have now. Go and talk to him and ask him to help you. He will lead you out of the fog." So off they went.

She told me of another man whom she had awakened. He was very disgruntled. He couldn't get out of the desert. He said "They tell us about harps and trumpets and now all we get is sand and desert."

"Pretend you've got a trumpet to blow."

"I'll try anything once if it helps—a trumpet—haven't had a trumpet since I was a kid. Here it is, I've got a trumpet, I've got a trumpet!"

"Friend, you've got to use your mind. You're in a place where you have to think things. Think of your dead relations and friends. Think *hard*."

"Blow me if it isn't the old man. What's he doing here? Blow me."

"Speak to him friend, and ask him to direct you."

"Thanks for the tip. I'll see you later."

Vale Owen. "Another made to understand. Thank God for your service. He'll be all right now and will lead some of the others away from the earth ..."

The last visit about which I propose to tell you was to a London medium in an effort to help a New Zealand Air Gunner who was lost and unhappy, but had been able to get a message through that channel.

With the help of Colonel Gascoigne we succeeded in making the contact, but the peculiar and distressing part of the episode consisted in the fact that the boy manifested in between the manifestations of two personating spirits.

The circle was obviously accustomed to this sort of thing and the boy was subjected to such a hail of queries and checks and tests that he became very sulky, and after saying that he had met the Colonel and would be all right now, refused to answer any more questions.

That same evening he came through to our own circle. I was telling L.L. how miserable the boy had been, when the Colonel said:

"The boy is not and was not half so miserable as he seemed." (He comes forward and speaks.) "I was miserable because they were so stupid. There was so much I wanted to tell you, but I didn't have a chance. We hear a lot about English manners down under, but I don't call it manners to invite a chap to meet you and then demand his identity disc."

L.L. "He wants to thank you for directing the Colonel towards him and for helping him to find his comrades again." "I have no regrets whatsoever for having left the earth, not even that I am out of the fighting, because I'm still on Operations with the Squadron. I've actually been flying again since I saw you this afternoon. 'Thank you' is very inadequate for what I feel, but it's the best I can do in words.

"I'll just go on flying and fighting with my comrades until we've swiped the Hun out of the skies."

Colonel Gascoigne. "It is a joy, it really is a joy, this work." This brings me to the question of false messages and personating spirits, it raises the question of the authenticity, the validity and the accuracy of the messages which are received from sources purporting to be discarnate.

In other words, is the alleged spirit a spirit? Is he the person he claims to be? Does he know what he is talking about? And can he get his message through without distortion? In many cases the answer to one or more of these questions is 'No.' This is why the path of Spiritualism is beset with so many pitfalls.

Not being a medium myself I cannot give a first-hand account of a medium's experiences, but I have already seen enough to convince me of the dangers to which people lay themselves open when they undertake, in a spirit of curiosity and sensationalism, and without due safeguards, to attempt conscious communication with discarnate spirits. Almost any half-dozen people, sitting round a table and putting their hands upon it, can generate enough power to make the table move, and perhaps to get recognisable answers to questions by means of an alphabetical code.

In many cases these people do in fact effect touch with discarnate spirits—but with what sort of spirits? Just the same idle and curious types as the sitters themselves. Remember the Law of Attraction, 'like goes to like.' The Lower Astral is full of loafers and idlers who are attracted by the invitational light given out by the sitters, who soon perhaps pick up some Joey or Sambo or Abdul who graciously consents to be their 'Guide,' and introduces them to as many Napoleons and Cleopatras and Shakespeares as they care to waste their time in listening to.

Sometimes, perhaps, some poor wandering spirit, in desperate need of help, may drift into one of these circles, and what help can they give him? It is the help of the Holy Spirit which he needs, and they do not have it to give. Is it likely that any of God's Ministers, engaged on the Master's work, would make contact with people actuated merely by motives of curiosity and sensationalism? Such people get what they bargain for (and sometimes more than they bargain for) and do much to discredit what is accepted as Spiritualism by rational and sensible people.

I don't for a moment suggest that earnest and unselfish people, genuinely seeking communication in order that they may be able to help others, can never make good and useful contacts by such methods (we may take Sir Oliver Lodge's circle as a case in point); but I should say that the principal factor influencing the result was that of *Motive*.

Now we come to the case of the individual who, finding perhaps accidentally that she has mediumistic powers, sets forth alone and uninstructed on the path of psychic self-development. (I use the feminine gender because there are more women mediums than men, and because women are more prone to take short cuts to their destination.)

Here again a high and selfless Motive may ensure a safe passage, but it is a dangerous road if lightly entered upon. I quote from the fourth and last article of a series which appeared under my name in the *Sunday Pictorial* in June 1943. "Who would go and sit in Hyde Park and share the secrets of her heart with the first stranger who chose to come and sit down beside her? And yet the amateur medium does that and worse, for the stranger may refuse to go away when he is no longer welcome.

"I have had two letters from people who are apparently possessed by alien personalities, and one from a medium who has escaped from this dreadful predicament.

"Another correspondent has sent me a typical piece of automatic writing which she produced while experimenting without guidance.

"It reads: " 'Wellington wants England win. You will give this message to Hugh Dowding. Wellington wants England win.'

"Now it is extremely probable that Wellington does want England to win, but perhaps less probable that he should have chosen this means of communicating his sentiments. I blame myself for not having included a warning against irresponsible 'Spirit Hunting' in my introductory remarks.

"For this flippancy I received a sharp rebuke from His Grace some ten days later.

"'How dare you say,' he wrote, 'that there is no guarantee that I am the Duke of Wellington? ... I am Mrs. X's Guide, and no spirits can enter without my permission. I want you to write to Mrs. X and apologise, and then we will forget all about it . . . I am very proud of my medium and have well tested her and am perfectly satisfied.' He went on to say that he proposed to write his life story in shorthand through the agency of a celebrated film actor who had recently lost his life in tragic circumstances. The letter ended up 'I will now wish you good afternoon and God bless you. Wellington of Waterloo.'"

Other parts of the letter were even sillier, but I do not think it fair to the poor woman to publish it in full; though of course I withhold her name. I would omit the story altogether if it did not afford such a very good object lesson.

I wrote to Mrs. X and pointed out how very unlikely it was that a great national figure, statesman and aristocrat, would write in such a style; but she would pay no heed to me.

Many other letters have I received from complete strangers, messages purporting to come from Sir Oliver Lodge, Sir Arthur Conan Doyle, Vale Owen, etc. The majority of these messages are spurious, though some have been authentic.

One of the main criticisms against Spiritualism has been that distinguished men are made to utter such fatuities after they are dead. The reply is of course that in the large majority of cases the distinguished man has had nothing to do with the messages attributed to him. To the distinguished person it must be a grim thought to imagine all the drivel and nonsense, which will be put into his mouth after he is dead.

Some self-styled mediums go on happily for years unconsciously sending themselves messages from their own submerged selves, under the impression that they are communicating with important personalities on the other side.

You may wonder why I, a mere neophyte on the path to knowledge, speak with such assurance of the credibility or otherwise of the messages which reach me from various sources. The answer is that, if the matter is important, I generally get what the Americans call the 'lowdown' from my friends on the other side.

For instance, it was important that I should be right about the Duke of Wellington, and this is what was given to us in that connection:

"We have been investigating, and there is an undeveloped but nonmalicious spirit with her, who would not be accepted if he gave his true identity—that of an Irish dock-labourer. We are helping him, and he is easier to deal with than she, who is in a welter of misunderstanding, pride and mock-humility."

But unless I get this kind of help I have no means of judging the authenticity of messages except my own common sense. Some of them are very plausible and I make no claim to be an authority on the subject.

One other thing, if you come across personating spirits in the course of your work, treat them gently and kindly. They are spirits as we are, and if they have halted in their journey towards the light, that is a matter for our compassion and not our anger. Our anger will hurt them " and that" (as Z says) "is not permissible."

There is another aspect of the phenomena of impersonation on which I have received help, and that is in the matter of 'Shades' and 'Shells.'

Some Theosophists believe that when man reaches the stage of what is called the Second Death, and relinquishes his astral body on leaving the Astral Sphere, this astral body retains some glimmering of mind stuff—just enough to enable it to continue a sort of semiconscious existence, and to manifest at séances, but without giving utterance to anything but the merest futilities. These are called Shades.

It is held that other astral bodies are completely empty and evacuated by their previous tenants, and that these can be actuated by Elemental spirits, and can manifest at stances under the pretence that they are still tenanted by their previous owners. These are called Shells.

This theory is expounded by C. W. Leadbeater in his book *A Text-book of Theosophy* and is strongly represented as fact by a section of Theosophists in California.

I was talking over this strange idea with L.L. after a sitting when Chang broke in:'

"Who *dares* to say that we are so careless of our discarded bodies as to allow such a thing to happen? You Earth-people die and leave your bodies for others to deal with; but, at the Second Death, we disintegrate our discarded bodies before we pass over, and reverently deliver back the residue to the source whence it came." I told him about the Leadbeater book, and he said, "Well, I thought I knew my astral pretty well, but I have never heard of such a thing. I will make enquiries and let you know later." Next week he confirmed his previously expressed opinion. He said that Shells did exist, but that they were lifeless thought-forms, created sometimes for ill purpose by those practising Black Magic on Earth (for Black Magic is a very real thing), and sometimes almost accidentally by a concentration of human thought on some prominent character in fiction (I thought of Sherlock Holmes). These latter are quite harmless.

It is rather important to remember this conversation. As I shall indicate later, I think that the Theosophists are probably as near to the Truth as any Religion or Philosophy—at any rate in the Western Hemisphere. The main point in which the teaching which I have received runs counter to theirs is in this question of mediumship. They discountenance and discourage it in every way, even to the extent of forbidding it, whereas I believe that, through selfless and dedicated mediumship, we shall attain to knowledge, which will expedite the coming of the Kingdom of Heaven on Earth.

On another evening L.L. had been reading a statement attributed to Madame Blavatsky, that Katie King was the last spirit which had spoken to mortal man, and that all who came after her were personating elementals. I said, "Did you ever hear such nonsense? Do you suppose that Z and Clarice are elementals? Clarice broke in "I'll elemental you!" and Z said, "Nothing is so hard to counter as a half-truth. I'll leave that for you to think over."

It is of course a great advantage to a medium in detecting personation if she is clairvoyant and can see the spirit with whom she is conversing.' The Astral being cannot imitate the radiance of the Angel, and the manipulator of the Shell can ignite no spark of life behind the eyes.

I was ruminating on the difficulties which beset the medium in distinguishing between the true and the false, when Chang said, "The best and only guard against personating spirits is unselfish desire to serve and to gain knowledge. It sounds simple. It is simple. But Man is complex, and often deludes himself that he is selfless. That is why all great teachers stress the need for prayer and self-searching truly to understand one's real motives."

The next question is "Do the spirits know what they are talking about?" and the answer in many cases is "No." There is no cataclysmic revelation of all knowledge at death, and the newly arrived spirit knows about nothing except his immediate surroundings, and is very often wrong about that, not because he wishes to deceive, but because he does not understand. He may not even know that he is dead, but, if he does, he knows little more than that he continues to exist (which he had not perhaps expected) and he knows whether he is happy or not.

Since all spirits continue to exist, and the majority are happy, the crude and ill-informed messages received from men killed in battle can be of the greatest value and comfort to their relations and friends on Earth, and incidentally to the spirits themselves, since the natural grief of the bereaved depresses the spirits and hampers them in their development. So they are helped by this little contact which makes them realise that, after all, they are not finally separated from earth conditions nor from their loved ones.

Furthermore, their messages, in spite of their inaccuracies in detail, are so vivid and graphic that they convey to the average mind better evidence of survival than do accounts of meticulously supervised sittings specially organised to counter the stock arguments of the sceptic.

Still, we obviously cannot expect to learn any deep truths about the hereafter from these young men, living, as they do, so largely among the creations of their own minds. If we can learn that they have set to work to help others, or that they have consented to go back to school to absorb the knowledge which is theirs for the asking, we shall know that they have escaped the danger of becoming Earth-bound idlers, and that all is well with them.

When it comes, however, to acquiring knowledge of the deeper truths of the hereafter as a guide for our conduct and for the edification of humanity, difficulties begin to arise. Broadly speaking, the greater the knowledge and development of the spirit, the more difficult it is for that spirit to communicate with Earth. The wavelengths of the spiritual ether have to be stepped down to our coarser vibrations, and this is a process requiring a good deal of cooperation and organisation. This is the work of Groups working under the directions of The Master (or of a Master, according to your way of looking at things) and, naturally, such a Group will select its earthly instruments with the greatest care; not only, nor indeed mainly, for the technical efficiency of the receiving station, but for the purity of motive of the recipients, and the use which they will make of the information when received.

It seems in a way presumptuous on our part to criticise any message or series of messages purporting to come from a high source. Every circle will naturally champion the claims of its own Guides to enlightenment and wisdom, but there are such astonishing divergences' in the teaching which is given to different circles by entities claiming equal authority, that the seeker after Truth is compelled to devise some form of test which will guide him in the difficult task of discrimination.

St. John gives us some good advice in the fourth chapter of his first Epistle. He says "Beloved, believe not every spirit, but try the spirits whether they are of God, because many false prophets are gone out into the world. Hereby know ye the Spirit of God. Every spirit that confesseth that Jesus Christ is come in the flesh is of God." As I say, this is good advice, but we shall need something more than this. There are many paths to the Top of the Hill and not all follow the Path of Jesus. Yet one, who follows the Tao or the Path of the Lord Buddha, if he has reached enlightenment, will recognise our Blessed Master and what He stands for.

The trouble is that there are many followers of Jesus Christ who yet have not attained unto full enlightenment. Some clergymen, for instance, begin broadcasting somewhat prematurely.

One of the signs of wisdom and enlightenment is humility. In Chapter 1, I quoted our dear Z. "I am a weak and lowly person, but the power vested in me is great. Lest it be sullied I must walk humbly."

And again, "I come to you as a friend, not as a counsellor, because my knowledge is little greater than your own. Remember we both serve; and together we shall exalt Him whom we serve. Mistake not the Messenger for the Master."

If one finds a tendency on the part of a communicating spirit to stress his own state of advancement and his self-sacrifice in devoting himself to mortal affairs, and if at the same time one finds high sentiments interlarded with mundane and material predictions, then one may perhaps suspect the presence of some Astral pretender, benevolent perhaps, but without the knowledge and authority to which he lays claim.

This may be the answer to the often-asked question "Why did the spirits say there would be no war?" The elevated spirits who alone are in a position to know do not disclose matters from which material advantage may be gained.

As a further test I think that we may add to St. John's dictum that other saying "By their fruits ye shall know them."

Here I should like to insert a short parenthesis on the subject of Prophecy. The word is loosely and inaccurately used as a synonym for Prediction. (I confess that I have myself made use of it in this sense.) Literally a Prophet is a mouthpiece for his inspiring deity - he is only incidentally a foreteller of the future. For example" Prophesy who is it that smote thee" said the soldiers who struck the blindfolded Jesus, not "who shall smite thee."

It seems to me an incontestable truth that (a) Prediction of an event, (b) Freewill, and (c) Disclosure of the prediction to the person concerned, are incompatibles.

For instance, if a predictor knows that I am going to be killed tomorrow in a railway accident and keeps his mouth shut, then I shall be duly killed on my way up to London. But if he tells me about it, I shall say "Very well then, I shall stay in bed all day. You may blow me up with a flying bomb, but I am not going to be killed in a railway accident."

This flippant example is really quite important because there are those who say that the past and the future are equally fixed on the scroll of time and that living in the present between the past and the future is only a mundane illusion.

Whatever such people may say, the future *can* be altered by the exercise of our freewill.

The Very Great ones may admittedly see into the future so accurately as to foresee the exact way in which each individual will exercise his freewill and so get an accurate picture of the whole.

But those who communicate with us are generally restricted to the prevision of tendencies, and this is where prediction may be useful and valuable to the progress of the world. For example: —A Statesman receives the message "If you adopt the existing draft plan for World collaboration for the maintenance of peace, it will fail because such and such a nation will be unable to tolerate restricted facilities for emigration." This is a fanciful example designed to show how individuals may be helped to exercise their freewill for a useful purpose.

On the other hand messages such as "The war will end in the West on March 18th, 1945" seems to me to be perfectly pointless, in addition to which they are generally wrong and bring much discredit on Spiritualism. Messages such as those, which predict the results of races, and so enable the recipients to obtain money by swindling others, are obviously noxious. They are either Black Magic or Poppycock - generally the latter.

Now for my last question "Can the Spirit get his message through without distortion?"

The answer depends on the power of the spirit, the means of communication and the receptivity of the medium. Spirits soon cease to think in words as we do. They think in pictures and thought-forms, and the medium clothes the pictures in her own words (except when the control is so deep that the medium is unconscious of what is coming through her). Accordingly, there is no doubt that some messages are materially distorted by the mind of the medium, or in some cases by the minds of the sitters.

This is a vast subject with which I cannot pretend to deal adequately in a book, which has to cover a wide field. One of the best books which I have read on mediumship is *Man's Latent Powers* by Phoebe Payne (Faber & Faber). Read it if you can get, hold of it.

I had to mention this problem of distortion, because I want to finish the chapter by reverting to the advice I gave in *Many Mansions* (after much searching of heart) to those who wanted to know whether they should initiate attempts at communications with their loved ones on the other side. The question was discussed on pages 98 and 99 and crystallised in the words, "Do not normally attempt to initiate communication from this side, but do not repel or resist a message or an impulse to receive a communication; accept it gladly." And now I have to consider whether, in the light of further knowledge, I still think this to be good advice.

And a year after the words were written I still have to say, "I don't know, I really don't know."

If a mother or a wife could be certain of making a true contact with her son or husband, I shouldn't have the slightest hesitation in recommending her to make it. But she cannot be sure.

I suppose I must have had at least three dozen letters from mothers and wives about their men, reading something like this. "John has been reported as missing and believed killed, but I know that he is safe. Two mediums have told me so. He is in a prison camp and has lost his memory—or—He escaped from his pursuers and is in hiding with the underground organisation—or—He is being sheltered by the monks in a Macedonian monastery, etc., etc. His grandfather came through and told us that he was not on the other side—or—the Guides say he is not with them, he is in a prison camp in a hot climate."

I do not for a moment say that none of these messages is true; I should like to think that they all were, but, so far as it is possible to be certain of anything of this sort, I am certain that some of them are false, because we have succeeded in making contact in some instances with the spirits of the men themselves and their messages have been accepted as authentic.

This state of affairs is infinitely distressing, and I have cast about in my mind for explanations. I can think of three, excluding a fourth, viz. deliberate dishonesty on the part of the medium, which I have no reason to suspect. But I do think it possible that in some cases the medium may subconsciously think, "If the boy were on the other side I am sure that I should make a contact. As I can make no contact, it follows that he is alive."

Probably the most common cause for the delusion is the desperate anxiety of the mother or wife that her man *shall* be alive. It must be very difficult for any but the most experienced medium to resist some form of thought-transference from such an intense mental concentration.

A third possibility (and one which may account for the appearance of the 'grandfather') is the intervention of personating spirits. These may be idle and foolish, but they are by no means necessarily unkindly. I think that perhaps one of these, seeing the poor woman's agony of mind, may intervene in the character of Guide or grandfather and give a message which brings comfort for the moment although in the long run it only adds to her pain.

There are other reasons too, which may prevent communication at the time chosen by the inquirer. Some souls spend quite a long time in sleep, and then have to be protected for a further time against Earth impacts, which they are not strong enough to bear.

A certain percentage of souls lose interest in affairs of the Earth almost immediately and go on into regions where the Earth-pull is not felt. And there are probably a dozen other reasons about which I know nothing. I am only trying to give you my little experience and am not setting myself up as an expert on this bewildering subject.

If you feel that you *must* try to make a contact in the early days following a loss, I should say: —Choose the best medium available, talk to your boy at night for two or three days before you pay your visit and tell him your intentions, take with you some personal article carried or worn a good deal by your boy and handled as little as possible by others (this will sometimes help in establishing a telephone line), empty your own mind as far as possible of strong thoughts and emotions, and abide by the result.

Don't go flitting about from medium to medium, that way lies confusion worse confounded.

And finally please don't write to me and ask me to recommend individual mediums, because I am sorry to say I cannot undertake to do so.

Paradoxically enough, the best and safest way to effect communication with your boy may be not to think about it at all, but to treat Spiritualism as a means of helping others—of giving rather than receiving. If you can take an opportunity of joining some little home circle as a regular member—a circle that is dedicated to the selfless service of humanity on both sides of the grave, it is more than possible that you will find yourself in communication with your boy, and perhaps actively engaged with him in the Master's work.

CHAPTER XII

REINCARNATION

And now I come to the subject of Reincarnation. In *Many Mansions* I left the subject very much in the air on account of the extraordinary diversity of teaching on the subject, which was given by various authorities.

I wrote, "It is astonishing! One would say that Reincarnation is either a fact or not a fact, and that there could not be two opinions about it on the other side. If it is a fact, there must be a continuous avalanche of spirits sliding back into earth-life and leaving gaps which must be noticeable by everyone, and if it is not a fact, how has the delusion spread so widely among the spirits closest to earth life and so, presumably, in the best position to watch what is going on?"

Well, now I want to tell you that I am personally convinced beyond any shadow of doubt that Reincarnation is a fact. I don't think that I can prove it as Survival can be proved, because the conviction has come to me as the result of personal revelations which are not for publication. Hitherto I have been given glimpses of six existences anterior to my present life, and I have little doubt that more will be revealed. Many of my friends, too, have received similar disclosures.

But these are given to us for a definite purpose, viz., that we shall realise the essential impermanence and unimportance of our present Personalities, in comparison with the persisting, enduring, immortal individualities which are our true selves.

Suppose, for instance, that I was once a Roman Centurion (which, so far as I am aware, I was not) it will help me to a true sense of values to realise that, in a century more or less, Hugh Dowding and Caius Sempronius will equally be 'has-beens' in the literal sense, but that the divine spark which animated both persists eternally, enriched by their experience but uncontaminated by their mistakes.

This information is not given to us for the purpose of self glorification or idle talk; though there are plenty of entities on the other side who are prepared to feed this sense of self-importance by supplying gratifying information on the subject *ad libitum.*

I have an amusing correspondent in America who writes from a small town in Vermont: —

"Even in this one-horse town there are, to my knowledge, four Cleopatras, who are not on speaking terms. Professional jealousy I suppose." I replied suggesting that it might be an educative activity to organise a National Convention of Cleopatras.

The information, when genuine, comes from what are known as the Akashic Records. One may think of these as cinematograph records which are stored away and can be drawn from the storehouse and exhibited by and to those who are permitted to have access to them. Actually, I think, the process is both simpler and more complicated. I believe that those who are given access to the Records move back in Time and see the actual events as they happened, or rather, see them happening.

I feel at liberty to give you one of these pictures since the identity of none of the actors is divulged.

The scene is laid in the temple of O YAT SEN near the frontier between China and Tibet, and the time? I don't know, but probably some time before the Christian era.

L.L. " Very beautiful Temple. Eastern. It is a large Temple with five Pagodas, one in the centre rising like a frail minaret, and four others, one at each corner. It is set in extensive and beautiful gardens. Near the Temple are courtyards. I feel that the priests and temple maidens live within the grounds. The immediate courtyard of the Temple is enclosed by a wall, not very high, and outside is a water garden, and beyond, the gardens and dwellings of the Temple servants. The inner courtyard is divided by small trees into three parts. The first partition is opposite the entrance and leads to the Temple. To the right is the dancing courtyard and the women seem to congregate there. To the left is a small partition where only the Priests may penetrate. There are five steps to the Temple entrance. The doorway is very beautiful, fine metal work and polished wood. A large brass gong hangs at the right of the door.

"The garden of the Women. They are practising dancing. They have long scarves or veils of different colours which they weave into lovely and intricate patterns as they move their hands. They stamp their feet gently but remain in the same spot. The rhythm is from the waist upwards and they bend in a most supple and fantastic manner. Now they have moved en bloc to change the pattern. They are wearing baggy trousers gathered at the ankles and pointed caps of gold and small breast plates of the same material. Feet are bare.

"The music is low pitched and seems to consist of cymbals and reed pipes.

"The scene is changing.

"Two dancing girls are in the outer courtyard of the Temple. They are wearing long dark cloaks and are moving round to a side door. As they reach it and are in the shadow of the doorway another girl comes running quietly up to them. She begs them not to go on. The eldest girl turns and accuses her of spying. She says no, she has dreamed she saw them lift the Veil on the Threshold and they were struck dead. She implores them not to go. The younger girl suggests they turn back as Flower has always been known as a true dreamer. But the elder girl is scornful. She is full of curiosity and wants to know what lies in the Hidden Place. She taunts the younger girl with cowardice and tells Flower to get away back to the Women's quarters. She takes the younger girl's hand and they go into the Temple.

"The lamps are burning dimly. They are made of exquisitely wrought metal. At the far end of the Temple a curtain is drawn. The girls make their way towards it. Quietly they slip behind it.

Before them is the Sacred Veil. It is a luminous sheet of iridescent colour.

"The younger girl is hanging back but the elder moves forward swiftly. She pulls aside the Veil. Inside is a small *empty* room.

"Now they are aware that they are no longer alone. A Priest has come through from the secret quarters. His face is terrible.

"Change of scene.

"I see a room with a large table shaped like a horse-shoe. The priests are seated round it and the two girls are standing before them.

The Chief Priest asks them if they have anything to say, if there is any reason that they should not suffer the death of a thousand flails or the bed-of red-hot nails? "

The elder girl speaks and agrees that the death penalty must be carried out, though she sees no reason why because she is doomed to wear the body of a woman, the light of the Shrine should be withheld from her. There is nothing behind the Veil, she cries in agony.

"The High Priest answers.

"'Curiosity never can see beyond Nothingness.' '

'The girl bows her head.

"'I had thought I sought enlightenment for my soul. You have pointed out to me my sin.'

"A young Priest rises up. The younger girl turns to him pleading.

He is known for his kindness, and gentle manner. He asks the elder girl to name her sin. The girl replies,' Curiosity.' "'Not that you have violated the Holy of Holies?'

"'No. My woman's body is an accident of birth but curiosity of mind is a sin of my soul, for that I shall pay. Let my sister remain alive. She did but follow me. I can bear torture for two.'

"The young Priest suggests that as the girl has the vision to see the real sin, the death penalty should not be carried out. He speaks earnestly to the High Priest.

"The girls are aware of a Love power and realise that Flower is still praying.

"The High Priest gives the verdict.

"'The soul imprisoned in female flesh has the lesson of female limitation to learn. To send it forth would be to destroy the purpose of the Gods. Therefore we decree that from henceforth, Amore shall be the meanest servant in the Temple kitchen. Heartsease, because she followed blindly, shall serve the dancing girls. There shall they learn true humility. That they shall not speak of what has transpired, their tongues shall be plucked out.'

"The young Priest showed many kindnesses to the two girls. When Chien passed on, Stoutheart became High Priest. Flower by her work and love became Head of the Dancing Girls, a position of great trust. Immediately she released Amore from the kitchen and put her to work with the Dancing Girls. When the new High Priest was chosen she prevailed upon him to allow the two girls to take part in the Temple ceremonies held in the outer court.

"During this life of physical silence, Amore developed the gift of the Spirit, and became aware while still in the bonds of matter, of the wider worlds and their inhabitants. Then was Chien sorrowful that he had made use of the letter of the law, for on his release he had much he would have liked to tell his brethren, and Amore could see and speak with him but could not tell what she saw, and because of her menial work could not read or write the characters of those days.

"Take heed then from this and let the Spirit dictate rather than the law of man when great issues are at stake.

"That Karma is over. Curiosity is burned out, and the time for seeing beyond the Veil of Nothingness is near at hand.

"BLESSING."

All the characters in this drama are known to me. Three of them are alive at the moment and two are dead. (It sounds funny when you put it like that, doesn't it?)

Most of what I shall write in the rest of this book is based on no better 'evidence' than the above. I accept it and believe it to be true, but I shall have no cause for complaint if other people do not.

It is difficult to define my feelings precisely, but I have a very deep affection for Z and Chang and others of the Group who are working so ceaselessly and selflessly to help poor distracted humanity in the name of the Most High. I know that they are real and true people; but I am not prepared to argue, or even to discuss the question with anyone on Earth.

They don't hand out knowledge and wisdom gratuitously. I have to work and read and think and ponder, and then I get a flash of illumination, perhaps from some quite unexpected quarter—a book, or a letter from a stranger. What they *do* promise is that they will keep me broadly on the right lines so long as I play my part, though I may get the details wrong. Z said to me once when I had made a mistake: —

"It is not my place to say to you 'this is so, and that is not so! You have asked me what you should learn from this.

I am going to answer very simply. 'Enthusiasm and Discrimination hand-in-hand lead to wisdom.' Does that satisfy you?"

(It seems difficult to exercise discrimination in matters where we have no data.)

"No. I am not being unfair. The pathway to Wisdom is no easy one. You will learn by your mistakes. But this I can promise —you will not teach falsely, though you may teach inaccurately."

The words 'Seek and ye shall find; knock and it shall be opened unto you' are as true now as on the day when they were spoken. But it is of no avail to seek with a vacant mind or to knock with empty hands.

And so I work with the Dear Ones in a spirit of love and trust and comradeship. What little knowledge I have gleaned I give to you freely. If it helps you, I am happy. If not, let it go. There is no royal road to wisdom.

A friend of mine recently sent me a poem by Geoffrey Winthrop Young entitled *For any Boy.* I quote the first verse. The mother speaks: —

"I wish him thought
That he may fashion faith even to a nought,
Rather than take another's creed on trust
And pass, a fool and profitless, to dust."

Now about Reincarnation. After due thought and study I asked Z. "Why is there so much contradiction in spirit messages about the truth or otherwise of Reincarnation?" He replied: —

"I can't say why there is this confusion, but I may offer an explanation of my own.

"At the time when the teachings of the Master Jesus were being prepared by men for the world, there were those among them who read His teachings to mean that He had freed them from the Wheel of Karma. Man is always desirous of finding a short cut. Hence, when the Teacher said 'I am come that ye might have Life,' they took it to mean an easy way of attaining the birthright of all Mankind—Immortality.

"So they withdrew the ancient knowledge that life must be refined and purified by the passage through many experiences.

"This teaching was such a solace to weary man that he steadfastly set his face against anything which would remind him of the necessity for labour, unfaltering untiring labour, in the purification of himself.

"Regarding the different teachings from our Spheres, many held that belief on the earliest plane—the Earth, and you must realise that we discard our beliefs only as we experience those things which show us how unnecessary they are.

"Many enlightened servants hold in their hearts a longing to be free from the wheel of Re-birth. Why? Because that is the ultimate destiny of all men. It is inherent in their very nature, this longing, for, having achieved exemption, the spirit is purified.

So many close themselves to this truth.

"Remember this. It is not important that you should be aware of previous lives or future lives. All that is important is that you realise that Man is greater than the manifestation of himself in physical matter. Also, if you accept personal responsibility, with all that that means, you no longer require to reincarnate.

"So, many of our friends emphasised and still emphasise the need for the full realisation of the Soul's responsibility to itself and others, and feel that this can best be brought about by looking forward. My friends and I feel it is better to try to visualise the whole, even inadequately, than to ignore a part because of that deep longing in our hearts.

"Another point is this. It is not usual for a personality to become aware of its connection with other personalities until egoic consciousness has been reached and linked with the outer manifestation of the Monad. It is not necessary to have passed physical death to reach this stage, but many have passed the first and second deaths, and even the third, without realisation coming upon them.

"In the lowest, which are closest to the highest, because of the Circle, very often a truth is understood. Here you will find many who know, I mean know, that they are not fit to be, free, and, because of that closeness to Reality which is the Ultimate, they are aware of this destiny.

"My brother, I am but imperfectly aware of these things and can only comprehend according to my knowledge and experience. That comprehension I freely give to you. But know that though you are incarnate and I discarnate, that is no reason to expect that my comprehension shall be greater than your own. So seek, and bring your reason to bear, and question me again."

If I may have the temerity to say so, I think that this is a very good explanation of the question which puzzled me while I was writing *Many Mansions*. There is another point also which explains itself in accordance with this message and my outline in Chapter IV. Souls do not normally reincarnate from the Astral, but pass through the second and third deaths before doing so, in order to dispose of their Astral and Mental bodies; their disappearance therefore is not noted as remark-able by the inhabitants of the Astral, as they appear to have gone 'on' in the normal manner, but their 'heaven life' is short and they are soon back on earth again. I think that, after the disappearance of the lower bodies, the Ego does probably have a considerable say in the choice of conditions in which it shall re-enter earth life. But the choice would be made in consultation with the Wise Ones of the heaven world, and the conditions would be such as to benefit the Individuality and not the new Personality. And so, when petulant young people say "I didn't ask to be born into this world" one thinks of the poet's aphorism:

'Even the youngest are not always wise.'

And another thing, it doesn't necessarily follow that rebirth will take place on this Earth. Do you remember the story of Ezra Martin where Z, in his explanation, used the words 'never to face death again'?

This puzzled me, and I asked Z "Is this the Law that those who pass through Hell are released from the wheel of rebirth? It was stated that the last of his five victims had now forgiven him. Is this also the Law? If so, is not the incidence of retribution very uneven?"

Z. "First concerning the innkeeper. He will not face physical death again in this evolutionary period. It was necessary for him to be confronted on his full awakening with the fact that each one of those he had wronged had fully forgiven him.

"One of those victims was an aristocrat who found it very difficult to forgive, not so much the taking of life, but the indignity of such a noble life being taken by a baser type. Also he felt that he himself had been negligent for one who had lived adventurously.

These are unimportant details to any but those concerned, but as you asked for enlightenment I give them to you.

"Before I pass on, is there any further question?"

("Do I understand that any soul after passing through Hell can reach perfection without again incarnating?")

"Not perfection. There comes a time in the evolution of a spirit when the *choice* of return, or of moving on to a different line of evolution is given. Knowing this soul, I know the choice he will make." Remember also that we do not always reincarnate in the same sex. It doesn't happen that I have been told of any of my female incarnations, but it would be very exceptional, I think, if I had experienced none. Some of my friends with whom I have been linked through the ages appear to have alternated between male and female with some regularity. We start on our long journey manifesting as happy beings without sex, but holding within ourselves all sex, and we shall return to that condition again. The marks of that duality remain on our bodies—but these are deep mysteries.

Again, some great Spirits, who have long passed the necessity to do so, incarnate selflessly for the love of poor humanity. We all know of One. And there is evidence that, in some instances, souls, particularly of children, may reincarnate immediately without any more delay than is demanded by the process of generation.

I do assure you that I write of these matters with the most profound humility. A little corner of the Veil has been lifted for me and I pass my knowledge on to you for what it is worth. But if you too are a seeker after Truth, you too must seek and read and ponder and discuss and evolve your own philosophy. For that is the only philosophy worth having. Of one thing only may you be reasonably sure, and that is that you will be wrong in some at least of your conclusions. But the habit of thought, the ploughing of the mind, the discarding of prejudices will serve you in good stead when one day you acquire your new-model intellect and are free to wander in the Fields of Wisdom, plucking the flowers which blossom there.

I have spoken of the Second Death, but hitherto I have given you nothing to convince you that it is anything more than an item in a scheme of philosophy which we must accept or reject on our own intellectual assessment of its inherent probability. Now I propose to give you an account of the actual ceremony as it was performed in one particular instance.

Shortly after I had been honoured by elevation to the peerage, I received the following message from Clarice:

L.L. "Clarice sometimes goes with Cushna to the outer edge of the Sphere where Z lives. She hopes before long to have an honour conferred upon her. She is hoping to make the transition to a higher condition. Cushna is helping her to become accustomed to the greater light. She is now on the outer verge of Summerland. 'Where I am going won't make much difference to our contact.

It is not a big change, but a definite step up.'"

Vale. "It isn't so little!' She has worked very hard for promotion. When the time comes to move up we will try to give you a record of her journey."

A fortnight later Z said "Our blessing upon you and we ask you to come with us in spirit to rejoice with us in the promotion of one who is dear to you."

The promotion of Clarice

L.L. "They are forming into groups, each group clothed in a different colour. Vale sends his greetings; he is leading a group clad in pearl-grey shot with blue. James (Lees) and Cushna are leading another group, rosy pink.

"There is a very broad pathway bordered with trees and flowers. The groups are coming in from the sides, and joining in the main stream down the centre. One group is in green. There is music but no singing yet. (L.L. joins the James and Cushna group.) They move at a steady pace. We are in a large meadow ('Oh! this is where I was last night' says L.L.) the grass is so beautiful; it is more like a huge lawn. There are many children in other groups.

"On the edge of the lake is a white platform glowing like alabaster. Steps lead up to it. Its whiteness reaches up and up. A group of four people is on the bottom step. Z is on the third step looking up; his robe is purple.

"Clarice and another girl are dressed in plain white. On the second step is another fine figure dressed like Z but in a golden cloak with clasps on the shoulders. (Later recognised as Lance, L.L.'s father.) The rest of the multitude are at the side of the steps. None below a certain spiritual level may stand on the steps or the platform. Groups of young people are singing and strewing flowers, alive and dewy.

"They are forming into the shape of a five-pointed star. Each point has a different colour. The fifth point is the shining path UP.

"A light appears in the distance, and approaches, there are forms and figures in the light. The entire concourse is bowing low.

Down the pathway of light comes a host of Shining Ones, stopping on the platform. One comes forward in a glorious light. He bids Z rise. Z mounts the steps and prostrates himself.

"The Shining One asks who is Sponsor for the two. Z says 'I sponsor both.' Lance places himself between the two and leads' them up. All stand before that wonderful figure bowing low. He blesses them.

"The two kneel at his feet. The sense of uplift and of glory is so very great. The Blessing, which comes from the Shining One, seems bound to pass right through everything down to the lowest sphere. Z takes one and Lance the other back into the bright group.

"Other steps lead down from the platform to the lake. The group goes down the steps, the rest go round. Everyone is singing; there are no words, just sound.

"Another group waits by the lake. They get into a boat like a gondola—a huge, barque. Instrumentalists are singing and playing. Now the Shining One is leading the two forward onto the barque. The rest gather round the lakeside. All quiet.

"Far off on the horizon is a rising Star. (Long silence from L.L. who seems unconscious.) As that Star rose, rays came across the water bringing a feeling of peace and beauty and glory. The whole multitude knelt.

"The boat moved out. Boats from other parts of the lake joined into the path of light. Waves of love came from those left on the edge.

"Music swelled and followed the boats. It seemed as if the music, like wind, wafted the boats along.

"They are GONE! All those happy ones, across the river of the Second Death into the joyous morning where the spirit can see and feel the Spirit of the Christ"

Vale. "We witnessed one group. There were many platforms.

Many aspirants being introduced to new teachers. Every boat had at least two aspirants."

Chang. "It is a great and glorious thing to leave the veils of illusion, leave the unreal, and start out on the quest of atonement with The Father. One day you too, even you, shall take part in this great joy. It may be a little while before Clarice will return; so much will open before her. She has left a thought of love like a jewel in my hand. I bring it to you now till she can tell you her experiences herself. Z has gone across the lake. If there are any questions, Vale will help."

(I asked some question concerning my father's recent doings.)

Vale. "Sorry, I can't help. Your father is not here tonight, but I can tell you where he is. He has gone with one of the parties on one of the accompanying boats. We can go and look in like travellers, but cannot enter higher Spheres. Your father is anxious to explore. Always when a group goes forward such an opportunity for exploration arises."

L.L. "Last night I was in the meadow lying on the grass. There were a great number of people there, many of whom I recognised. I saw that we were building the platform. All the little boats were brought to the edge and beached ready for use. I saw P. and C. and you. When the platform had been raised we all sat down; some had been bathing. A Teacher came, walking among the people and talking of service and brotherly love."

One of the subjects on which I was rather hazy when I wrote *Many Mansions* was the question of the future life of animals. Clarice knew that I was interested in this, and, being herself a devoted lover of animals, she undertook to make a special effort to help me in this matter. She was telling me about a little school of which she was in charge:

"I have twelve children under my care. All little mites - five boys and seven girls. I teach them by taking them into the woods.

"It is so wonderful, the complete understanding between us and animals and birds. There is no fear here, we are one big family. Becky (her King Charles Spaniel) plays with the children. She is still amiable.

"Some people say there are no animals 'Far On'; I can't believe that. Surely even in the Highest Heaven a bird must sing or a dog bark. They are part of the Creator, just as we are. It can't be just my love. Surely they must be there."

(Oughtn't they themselves to be progressing?)

"How do we know that there aren't; higher forms of animal life? What about flowers? Aren't they part of God too? I will find out. I can travel quite a long way inward now, and I'll go as far as I can and find out where they leave off."

About a fortnight later we received the following:

Clarice. "There are animals everywhere—right into the celestial spheres, at least what are celestial to me. I have found them everywhere.

"There is one place which seems to belong to them alone. None of us lives there. I went with a friend to visit them. We had to cross a 'space'; it was like a void. It is so hard to find the correct word. That is the best I can do—a void. Then we were among them.

"It is a rather beautiful place in its way. Great crags and ravines and woods and rivers, I saw lions and leopards and many wild beasts. They were all quite 'tame' and did not seem to mind us. One beautiful cheetah even followed me round.

"The birds are so lovely I find it difficult to describe them and their song so clear and exquisite; it is sheer joy to listen."

"Beautiful trees and flowers are everywhere, and butterflies and all winged creatures.

"My friend showed me a valley where there were some strange animals, some so beautiful in form and so graceful in movement one felt spellbound. These are some of the earth's future inhabitants, I was told.

"Domestic animals were there too, dogs and cats and horses.

All happy together, but any animal which is greatly loved by one of us seems to be much finer in every way than his fellows. I mean that he *looks* finer too—more graceful, shinier coat, more alert.

"Pets (which can only become pets by mutual love and consent) can live with us. I have my two dogs and a cat and three horses near to me. I seem to collect them somehow.

"In my search for the animals I went as far as I could reach into the Light and I found them all the way. But only the pets. The farther they are from their own place, the more they depend on their Love Guardian.

"My friend told me that they only exist on the Inner Planes because of the Love Bond.

"One great Shining One has a beautiful leopard as his companion. My friend told me the leopard had once saved His earth life, a long time ago, and the 'tamed animal' of those long-ago days has never been separated from the love of his Guardian.

"Another friend in the 5th Sphere from Earth has a gazelle as a pet, and another a beautiful Borzoi. Dogs are more plentiful, I find, than any other animal, lots and lots of small ones. There are a lot of cats too.

"One thing I noticed that the animals in the Inner Planes seem larger than their prototypes elsewhere. Pekingese for instance are quite large dogs. Love is the secret of their growth.

"I'm so happy to find them so far on the journey.

"Can you guess who my dear friend and helper on this journey was? You ought to!"

It wasn't very difficult to guess the answer to her last question.

The guide, of course, was Z.

Constantly during our talks we keep getting little allusions to pets and their co-existence with humanity after this life. L.L. had a beautiful black cat called Winston. The other day, during a 'Rat Week,' he picked up some poison and was found dead in the garden. That evening Clarice came to L.L. with Winston in her arms, just to show that he was all right.

I now see that the question I asked, inferring that we might hinder the progress of animals by keeping them with us after death, was a stupid one.

Humanity has a definite responsibility towards the higher animals, and association with humanity is one of the ways by which the animal soul elevates itself toward the possibility of attaining human incarnation. The cruel exploitation of animals is, I think, a greater sin than most people realise. The retention of pets after death, so far from retarding their progress, probably saves them from numerous incarnations.

Lovers of animals may like to read a book called *Hero by Heather* in which a dog speaks from the place where it is now living with its young master.

I will finish this chapter with an effort to reconcile the almost hopeless jumble, which the varied vocabularies of different communicators have created in our conception of the system of Spheres or Planes in which we shall find ourselves after physical death.

I made a very amateurish effort to cope with the subject in Chapter VIII of *Many Mansions*; and if I think that I can improve on that effort a little now, I do not infer that I am much nearer to the truth, but only that my ignorance may be a little less profound!

In the interests of clarity I should say that I propose to refer to the greater stages of progress as Spheres, and to Planes as being subdivisions of Spheres. This, though not in strict accordance with Theosophical ideas, will nevertheless serve to eliminate one of the major causes of confusion.

I asked Z for a reconciliation of the several nomenclatures of the Spheres, particularly between the Theosophical and that employed in Vale Owen's book.

Z. "It is simple. Regarding the book you mention, I can only suggest that the word Plane might be substituted for Sphere, a Plane being a division of a Sphere. Here is an excellent example of the reason why we are so desirous that L.L. shall provide us with a vocabulary from which we can choose words to give explicit meaning.

"Beyond the Fourth Sphere very little, if anything, can be comprehended by incarnate man. In the Fifth Sphere resides He whom you call Jesus, and the glory and the peace of that are beyond a description. Heartsease has passed the Second Death. Has it been explained to you what that means? (Yes.)

"The Astral is the Sphere of Illusion. The passing of the Second Death brings the first glimpse of Reality, when the soul becomes aware that all Creation is part of itself, as the soul is part of Creation. To realise this truth, even dimly, is a great step forward, but when it becomes in truth a reality, it brings a joy passing all understanding of those still bound by physical matter.

"You must realise that all these Planes and Spheres are but states of being. You can inhabit all of them at once, as I do. But to do this one must strive, one must be prepared to serve Him.

"The usual method of unfoldment of understanding is exceedingly slow; it takes thousands of years, because after each death, in each Personality-life, only a fragment of understanding can be vouchsafed. But each succeeding passing adds another fragment to the whole, until you (the personality) become so evolved that you are capable of speeding-up the process and withstanding the increased pressure. This is so important that I must pause and ask you, have I made it clear?"

(Not quite. Clarice spoke of a woman with a gazelle in the Fifth Sphere. Where would that be?) "Heartsease is with us in the First Plane of the Third Sphere.

It may be that you would call it the Lower Mental. The gazelle was in the Second Plane beyond the Astral.

"The Earth has three Astral Planes above it and two below it (with one the lowest of all). The Christ Sphere is the Fifth Sphere.

Jesus manifests on the Fourth Sphere. His home is on the First Plane of the Fifth Sphere.

"The Sixth Sphere is one which we dimly comprehend—beyond that, not at all."

The human brain cries out always for precision, and so I have tried (with all due apologies for attempting to define the indefinable) to set out in tabular form three comparative tables of the Spheres.

I have chosen three authorities. Z, for I naturally tend to give my own credence to his teaching. Vale Owen - for I used his system to illustrate *Many Mansions*. And the Theosophists, for they claim to speak with authority on the subject.

If you have a pet system of your own, it may interest you to make a fourth column and see how it fits in with the dicta of the three authorities whom I have quoted.

Z Spheres and Planes	Theosophists* Planes and Sub-planes	Vale Owen Spheres
Seventh Sphere Seven Planes Nothing known	Divine Plane Seven Sub-planes	Unknown number of Spheres
Sixth Sphere Seven Planes Dimly understood	Monadic Plane Seven Sub-planes	

Fifth (Christ) Sphere
Seven Planes
First Plane, home of
  Jesus
	Spiritual Plane
	Seven Sub-planes
	
	Nirvana
		14 Christ Sphere above
		     this

Fourth Sphere Seven Planes Jesus manifests	Intuitional Plane Seven Sub-planes Plane of Buddhi	13 12 11
Third (Mental) Sphere 7 6 5 4 Third death 3 2 1 Second death	Mental Plane 1 ⎫ 2 ⎬ Upper Heaven 3 ⎭ 4 ⎫ Third death 5 6 ⎰ Lower Heaven 7 ⎱ Second death	10 Last Sphere in touch with Earth 9 8 7 6 5 Parting of the ways 4
Second (Astral) Sphere 7 6 5 4 First (Earth) Sphere 3 2 1 Hell	Astral Plane 1 ⎫ 2 ⎬ Summerland 3 ⎭ 4 ⎫ 5 ⎬ Purgatory 6 ⎭ 7 Hell	3 2 Newly arrived souls 1 Earth Hell
	Physical Plane ⎰1 Atomic 2 Sub-atomic 3 Super-etheric ⎨4 Etheric 5 Gaseous 6 Liquid ⎱7 Solid	

* First principles of Theosophy, page 126

142

CHAPTER XIII

RELIGION

My intention has been, as I have said, in this book to set forth some of my own experiences, instead of recording the experiences of others, as I did in *Many Mansions*.

I do wish, however, to bring to notice a number of other aspects of the truth upon which I await further enlightenment.

I could of course write at length on these matters, quoting the experience and the opinions of others, but that is not my intention now.

Nevertheless, I should leave this present work very incomplete if I were to pass these things over in silence, for I am convinced that they are of the greatest importance.

Historically speaking, I think it to be a most remarkable circumstance that Institutional Christianity should have succeeded so thoroughly in suppressing amongst its adherents so much of the knowledge which existed in the world before the birth of Jesus.

Some brilliant brain once coined the aphorism "Culture is what remains after you have forgotten everything you learned at school" and as a cultured Englishman (in that sense) my religious teaching left me with a vague impression that before the year o the world existed in a state of complete spiritual darkness and ignorance, and that the only records of earlier conditions in which we could place any reliance were those of the Hebrew tribes.

My own spiritual pastors and masters, it is true, were inclined to allow me a little latitude in the strict interpretation of the account of the Creation and the story of the Garden of Eden; but there were (and are) others who are less liberal, and demand a literal acceptance of every word contained in the Bible.

The wisdom of the East—of India, of Persia, of Mesopotamia, of Egypt—was represented (in so far as it was referred to at all) as ignorant heathenism, "bowing down to wood and stone." All the billions who had died before the Gospel began to be preached were writhing in the torments of Hell, their first hope dawning when Jesus visited that region after His Crucifixion. Obviously some special dispensation must have existed for people like Abraham, Moses and Elijah, and possibly for all who had believed devoutly in Jehovah; but all that was left conveniently indefinite.

I believe that it is now historically accepted that the Old Testament was written by Ezra and his scribes about 500 years before the birth of Jesus, and finished at a later date by Malachi. The data available to Ezra must have degenerated by his time into folklore and tradition, except in so far as he may have been helped by direct inspiration.

But, setting aside the accuracy or inaccuracy of Ezra's record of his tribal legends, my point is that acceptance of the Book of Genesis, or in fact of the historical truth of the Old Testament generally, has nothing whatever to do with Christianity.

We know that the Universe was created by some Power, and that included in the Universe was this trumpery little planet; we also know that at some time and in some fashion organised Life appeared on Earth, and that Man is a part of that Life. These are matters of *fact*. There is a true explanation and a large number of other theories of various degrees of falsity. These things happened millions of years before the birth of Jesus; His coming could not make false true or true false, and it is a monumental achievement on the part of the early Church fathers that they succeeded in imposing this flagrant *non-sequitur* on Mankind, viz. that to be a Christian a man must accept the archaic records of the people who murdered Jesus Christ.

They did it, of course, by burning every book of the ancient wisdom on which, they could lay their hands, and by persecuting all those (as for instance the Gnostics) who held to former aspects of the ultimate truth. Such an achievement would of course be quite impossible nowadays, but it was not quite so difficult before the general spread of education and the introduction of the printing press.

They were not even consistent. They released the people from the law of Moses and from circumcision, and they shifted the Sabbath Day, but they held them to the Ten Commandments (nine of which are negative) in the place of Jesus Christ's positive injunctions to love and forgiveness and charity; and, in particular, they tied them to one of the least enlightened accounts of Creation and Evolution which were in existence at that time.

The wisdom of Egypt and of the Middle East was substantially obliterated; but fortunately their influence did not extend to India and the Far East, and it is thither that we must turn our eyes if we wish to resuscitate the knowledge which they so successfully eliminated in the West.

Not that there is now, or ever was within historical memory, any script or scripts containing the Naked Truth. That would be much too dangerous; and from time immemorial the Truth has been wrapped up in parable and allegory to which the keys were held only by the initiated priesthood.

It is of course true that the Old Testament stories are presented in similar guise, and there are other Hebrew books and Hebrew keys which elucidate them for those capable of pursuing the quest.

But the result of such pursuit is to link up Abraham with the Hindu scriptures, and to achieve a number of similar results highly disconcerting to orthodox Theology.

If we disentangle the Bible accounts of Creation and Evolution from the present underlying assumption of orthodox Christianity that it is wicked to question them, we are free to indulge in a very interesting comparative examination of alternative theories such as those which are propounded by Hindus, Buddhists, Rosicrucians, Theosophists and the like. Among very great differences of detail we shall find a strong parallelism in essentials, and we may not even reject the idea that these are all versions of the same story, which have diverged from one another partly because of the different channels through which they have 'descended, and partly on account of the differing disguises in which the initiated adepts have wrapped them up.

If you have nothing else to do and a lifetime to do it in, and if you don't mind starting your work by learning Sanskrit and Pali you will probably find the Hindu scriptures the most fruitful field. Even then you should be prepared to go and live in India and cultivate the acquaintance and friendship of the Brahmin and Buddhist priesthood. Few of my readers perhaps will possess the leisure, the opportunity and the inclination to embark on such a programme.

If you have about a year to spare, you may acquire a fair nodding acquaintance with your subject by reading the monumental works of

Madame Blavatsky, *Isis Unveiled* and *The Secret Doctrine*. These are very remarkable volumes, but they cannot be classified as light literature in any sense of the word. Parts of them are completely unintelligible to my limited brain, but parts are deeply interesting, and parts highly entertaining, especially when she lays her lance in rest against Theologians and Scientists. It is incredible that one woman's brain could hold so much learning—or rather it would be incredible if she were more the authoress and less the instrument.

But you—you ordinary person for whom I am writing—will probably not be able to find time to read these books even if you can procure copies. To you I would say, "Read a little about Theosophy." Now I want to make it quite clear that I am not a Theosophist, I am a Dowding-ist if I am any kind of an -ist at all. But I do believe that the Theosophists are nearer to the truth than any other Western creed or sect of which I have heard. I say this not so much because I trust my own power of judgment, but because the little doles of information from the other side which we get in our circle from time to time so often fit into the Theosophical picture, and into no other frame.

The book which I should recommend for you to read is *First Principles of Theosophy* by C. Jinarajadasa, or *Textbook of Theosophy* by C. W. Leadbeater.

I must warn you about one or two things if your study of Theosophy is to be only cursory. The first is that the attitude of the Theosophist is one of rather lofty indifference. He does not proselytise. Far from it. He says in effect "This is the Truth, at which we have arrived as the result of much, study and of investigation made by our seers. We present it to you, if you like, as a working hypothesis; but we are not prepared to argue about it. If you care to join our ranks and to learn from us, you will eventually discover for yourself that it is all true; but this consummation may not be reached in this incarnation; in fact it will probably occupy several lifetimes."

This is worse than my first suggestion that you should learn Oriental languages and go to live in India, because, as things are, you may very probably fail to bring through to your next incarnation the memory of your high resolve, and thus expend a good deal of energy without attaining to the intellectual conviction of which you are in search. Also, of course, this attitude is justifiable only if all their seers see the same things.

Next, if you have been brought up in Institutional Christianity, your ingrained ideas concerning Jesus and The Christ will receive a rude shock.

You will have to envisage Jesus as one of a number of exceptionally pure and perfect souls who was over-shadowed during His life on Earth by the Christ Spirit. You must be prepared to envisage the idea that between Jesus and The Absolute exist certain intermediaries. Apart from our own preconceived ideas, there is nothing irrational in this, in fact it would be contrary to our ideas of organisation if the Almighty Ruler of innumerable galaxies had no intermediaries between Himself and One who came as a Saviour to our inconsiderable planet. To adopt a homely simile, it would be infinitely less unpractical that a Commander in Chief should attempt himself to command every platoon in his group of armies.

Another point on which you, if you happen to be an altruistic Spiritualist, will find yourself in sharp disagreement with most Theosophists is in the matter of their attitude towards mediumship.

This is so hostile that, in some cases, members of the higher grades are forbidden to work with mediums.

This, in fact, is my own sharpest disagreement with a philosophy which I believe, on the whole, to be almost as near to the truth as contemporary man is likely to attain. I fully see the reason which makes this ruling politically wise. It aims at the prevention of schism due to the continual claims of mediums to have received revelations running counter to the dicta of accepted Theosophical seers. Some Theosophists say that all mediumship is false and that no discarnate souls can communicate with incarnate humanity; that everything received comes from mischievous, non-human, elemental spirits.

To no reader of this book need I explain how violently I reject such an assertion.

I don't propose here to attempt to write a summarised manual of Theosophy; I only wish to tell you what sort of information you may expect to find presented for your examination if you read something about the subject.

To begin at the beginning, you will find an account of the beginnings of organisation in Chaos, which we call Creation. We are told that the Solar System is an even more complicated mechanism than we think it to be, since it contains a number of planets in form invisible to us, existing as they do on the Astral and higher levels.

The evolution of life and form, the history of the present and past human races, a forecast of races to come, and the rise and fall of civilisations—all these are dealt with.

The laws of Reincarnation are given in such detail that one almost suspects them of being over-simplified; and the law of Karma, that is to say the great cosmic law of Cause and Effect, is outlined with similar precision.

Then, of course, the various Spheres and Planes of the Solar System, and of the infinitely greater Cosmic System which exists in the beyond, are described so far as description is possible (but the word 'Sphere' is not used in this connection; they speak of Planes and Sub-Planes).

An account is given of the invisible and non-human ladder of life, ranging from the gnomes and fairies Up to the great angelic beings, or Devas, which constitute their highest embodiment. We are also told of the evolution of visible life from the mineral to the plant, from the plant to the animal, and from the animal to the human.

Theosophy has of course, as its name implies, an explanation to offer concerning the nature of the Divine, It tells us that there is a Cosmic Logos Who embraces the entire Universe, and that a part of Him exists as the Logos of the Solar System, Who is the Being known and worshipped by us as God; that the Solar Logos has three aspects, corresponding to the Trinity which exists in various forms in most religions, and that under the Solar Logos operate seven Planetary Logoi, corresponding to the Christian conception of the 'Seven Spirits before the Throne of God.' These Planetary Logoi are the heads of the Seven Rays, of which I shall have more to say shortly.

The whole of Solar matter, physical and superphysical, is created out of bubbles in the ether by the will of the Logos, and is continued in existence solely by His will. It is organised by the Third Aspect of the Logos, it is vitalised by the Second Aspect and it is spiritualised by the First Aspect.

It is stated that there are seven grades of *physical* matter, four of them unknown to science.

The seven grades are solid, liquid, gaseous, etheric, super-etheric, sub-atomic, and atomic. The ultimate physical atom is a spiral form of incredible complexity, and there are eighteen of these in a single atom of Hydrogen (as known to our Scientists), while there are over one thousand in an atom of Uranium. These discoveries were made by clairvoyant investigation by Annie Besant and C. W. Leadbeater and are given in detail in their book *Occult Chemistry*. Then we are told of the Inner Government of the World, of the Great White Brotherhood, and the great Angel Lords who preside over the Seven Rays, of the Masters, of the Path and of Discipleship. These last things I *know* to be true, so far as any human being can say that he knows anything.

Hence the title of this book. In this connection I feel a trifle apologetic towards Clarice, who gave me the title "Once I believed, now I know." This failed to appeal to me owing to its lack of snappiness, and for a time I intended to call it "Now I Know." But that seemed to smack of arrogance, and was patently untrue except as concerning the bare facts of Survival and Progress. So I decided to call it "—The Entrance to the Path."

Now please don't imagine that I accept as literally true some of the materialistic accounts of the continuous physical existence of Masters on Earth.

When C. W. Leadbeater, for instance, tells us of the Master Christ living in a material body in Tibet, and the Master Jesus existing simultaneously in a physical body in the Jebel Druse, my intellect rebels. I am reminded bf the riddle "How does a sailor know there's a man in the moon?" And the answer is "Because he's been to sea."

Leadbeater tells us that he has seen, and even gives us a picture of Masters engaged in earthly avocations. But even so—

I mention this because it would be a thousand pities if anyone were deterred from a study of the framework of Theosophical teaching by a revulsion from any of the details. Remember that Theosophy is broadly based on the Ancient Mysteries. It is the best exposition of them which I know of as being available to Western Europeans. It may possess faulty keys to some of the caskets in which wisdom has been concealed; and, in so far as it depends on the revelations of its own seers, those seers were human men and women, and have not been guaranteed against error by any process of which I am aware.

I have not mentioned the Aura and the vortices (called the Chakras) in the aura which form channels connecting with vibrational influences outside the Personality. You will not find these mentioned in all Theosophical books, though specialised works on these subjects are readily obtainable. Information can also be obtained from Phoebe Payne's book *Man's Extended Powers*, which I have already recommended for study.

Reverting now to the Seven Rays. I think that this is a most important subject, and I only wish that I knew more about it myself, I have tried, to read one or two books about it, but they were full of long words which I didn't understand and I "came out by that same door where in I went." The broad conception is simple enough, viz., that Celestial Light is split up into seven components which are called Rays, and each Ray has seven sub-rays.

The Rays are associated with certain qualities and varieties of philosophical study, as follows: —

First Ray. The Divine Ray. The Ray of pure will power.

Second Ray. The Teachers' Ray. The Ray of the intellect.

Third Ray. The Astrological Ray. The Ray of times and of seasons, of choosing the appropriate moment to perform any act.

Fourth Ray. The Ray of physical perfection, of the control of the body and its attributes. The Artists' Ray.

Fifth Ray. The Scientists' Ray. The Ray of physicians and alchemists.

Sixth Ray. The Ray of pure devotion, of attaining resets by means of worship and prayer. The Ray in particular of the devout Christian.

Seventh Ray. The Magic Ray. The Ray of ceremonies and sacraments, of charms and invocations.

The idea is that each one of us works on one or other of the Rays, and perhaps on the sub-rays corresponding to other main divisions, and that, before we become perfect, we must learn to work on all the Rays. But exactly what 'Working on a Ray' means, and how it is done, I do not know.

Nor can I tell you of what type of etheric substance each ray is composed, nor how it differs from its fellows in colour, wavelength, or other attributes. I have a general idea that the First Ray is Golden, the Second Blue, and the Sixth Rose Colour, but I am quite probably wrong about this.

The reason why I think the subject to be important is that I believe that most forms of Spiritual Healing are effected, consciously or otherwise, by means of the Rays, and not only that, but that almost all transference of thought and power is carried out by means of the Rays. The experiments of which I wrote in Chapter VIII are feeble gropings into the nature and functions of the Rays.

Power Rays exist in the Earth and outside the Earth, and on the Earth in special storage-places. Glastonbury, Iona and Fuji Yama are instances of these. Colonel Gascoigne is deeply interested in this subject, and so also are my own People.

Readers of the *Letters from Lancelot* (recommended in *Many Mansions*) will remember that Lancelot received special instruction in the bending of Rays by means of 'keys.' He and his brother Christopher (killed in this war) have made a special expedition to Mars to collect such keys, which are apparently to be found there in large numbers.

In July 1943, L.L. said, "Clarice is plaiting some ribbons. No, they are not ribbons, they are little rays." *Clarice.* "They are little rays which I am learning to use. Z says they are offshoots of the Cosmic Rays. When I can handle these well I'll be able to take my place among the workers who direct the great Power Rays. I'll tell you about that, too.

"I am plaiting these as an experiment. We are told that the violet ray holds great spiritual healing and that the blue ray has physical healing power. I am plaiting them to direct to-night on an old man while he is asleep, to try and cure both spirit and body."

(She told us later that the experiment was successful.)

Colonel Gascoigne writes through his daughter: —

"Now you want to know about St. George. Well, he is our direct leader; all of us in the air are in immediate touch with his lines of force and direction. We are living in the fire of his being, the grace and ardour of his spirit. We are the sons of his mind and inspiration; he is the living force behind our success.

"So, when you ask whether your friend is under the influence of St. George, the answer is that he is more than that. He is a son of the ray of the St. George power. The ray covers all those who fight or die in order that happiness may come to others through their sacrifice; that is the note of St. George. He works upon the physical ray, which is red, turning it to rose colour, the ray of Love, Forgiveness, Gentleness and Sacrifice.

"Your friend is among those whose body now holds the ray, even as he has held it for many years. That ray is binding you can never be separated from those who bear its vibration in the blood.

"You are finding now that people have different types of blood. These can be altered by the continuous influence of thought setting up an action in the blood drawing us into the initiating influence of the St. George ray, and so into the order of Knighthood, the most Christ like so far known on Earth.

"Christ used the St. George ray by which to overcome death. It stands for us as the gateway of Resurrection. Sacrifice means death, either of the body or of the desires of life in some form. The Gateway to the Temple of St. George lies beyond the fulfilment of Love and the award of Sacrifice."

This message is of course puzzling if we imagine that this particular ray did not exist before St. George. It is a cosmic phenomenon and has existed since the beginning of time. It only means that St. George is the individual who is at present in charge of its operation. In due course he will pass on to higher work and another will take his place.

I have dealt with the Rays thus at length because I believe that they are enormously important to us. I believe that they are the vehicles of effective unselfish Prayer, and that by virtue of the Rays we live and move and have our being, the crops grow and the flowers bloom.

But whatever may be the truth, we have certainly much to learn.

I will conclude this somewhat disjointed chapter with a few words on Hell.

A good many readers of *Many Mansions* seem to have found Arnel's story unduly materialistic, and I must say that I had the same general impression. Of what use could be swords and armour and metal dug from mines, and why should souls exist in such terror of the pains of the body when they no longer possess physical bodies to be cut and lacerated and burned? We have received no direct teaching in our circle on conditions in Hell, but I have recently read another book on the subject which has made all these things appear in a more reasonable light. The book is Volume II of *Gone West* by Ward (Psychic Book Club).

It relates the experiences of an army officer who passed rapidly downwards through the Hells to the Bottomless Pit and thence struggled slowly upwards again.

If you read this book you must make allowance for the fact that the terminology employed is quite different from that which I have adopted as standard. In particular, what I have called the Etheric Double is referred to as the Astral Body, and there are other differences which tend to cause confusion.

When allowances have been made for these divergences, the story bears out other accounts in the impression of actuality which exists in the minds of the sufferers. All pain is ultimately mental and these poor creatures feel pain as they do on earth as they are cut and lashed and burned.

The strongest reigns by his will-power, but "uneasy lies the head . . .," because he is subject to a never-ending series of conspiracies among his subjects, and he can never dispose of his enemies by killing them, he 'can only torture them, which still further inflames their mutual hatred.

All loot and plunder disappears as soon as seized; there is in fact no enjoyment of anything.

Further light is thrown upon obsession and Black Magic and the conditions in which evil spirits are enabled to manifest and to trouble mankind. One illuminating thought is that there is no need to employ Devils, that is to say entities that have never been human, except in the lowest depths. Man's inhumanity to man is all that is required above those levels. He with the stronger will oppresses and tortures the weaker, but there must naturally be some superhuman force to oppress and torture the strongest mortals when they reach the lowest depths or else there would be nothing to prevent these strong ones from stagnating eternally in the pit.

I have an idea that these inhuman monsters are created out of Elemental Essence on its journey downwards into mineral life, and therefore that even these Devils are in a state of progress in accordance with the laws of evolution.

I may be wrong about this, very likely I am. Perhaps we are not intended to know too much about the Hells, or to speculate too deeply on the subject. In any case we know quite enough to realise that Hell very definitely exists and that it is a very good state to avoid.

CHAPTER XIV

CLOSING THOUGHTS

In the light of my present knowledge the chapter in *Many Mansions* with which I am least satisfied is the last one, which I called "The impact of Spiritualism on Religion."

Perhaps the inadequacy of my treatment of the subject was not altogether my fault, because it was not, and is not, too easy to determine the Highest Common Factor in the very diverse beliefs professed by Spiritualists as a whole. Some hold to Reincarnation, while others reject it, some keep Jesus Christ as the heart and core of their faith, while others reject Him and carefully excise His Name from the hymns which are sung at their services, and some treat spirit communication as a subject for scientific study without paying any attention to its possible impact on the life and conduct of humanity.

This is why I have said, and still maintain, that Spiritualism is not a Religion. It is too young, too experimental a movement to have settled into a groove narrow enough to justify such a definition. Nevertheless Spiritualism may be Religion, which is a distinction not without a difference. And I believe that it will be one of the most important stepping-stones towards the unification of all the important religions of the Earth into an eventual World Religion.

I ask leave now to make a short digression to discuss the general question of talking about religion in ordinary society. It is just one of those things which is Not Done except by parsons and outsiders.

It is one of my handicaps that I have a retentive memory for dog-gerel, but I can never remember its context. If I wrongly accuse A. P. Herbert of responsibility for the following, will he forgive me?

"As my old father used to say
When parsons came to call
He's not my sort, but pass the port
Thank God there's room for all."

I told you in Chapter XI of our dealings with the *soi-disant* Iron Duke; but I did not tell you of a visit we had from the genuine 6th Duke of Wellington who was killed in a very gallant Commando raid in Sicily. He came to give a message to his relations, and that message is no concern of ours, but he had quite a little chat with me, and what he said is germane to our present subject.

He said "Why don't all you people believe in survival, and why weren't we told about it?"

(That is the cry, repeated again and again by fighting men, parsons, labourers and people of all classes—"Why weren't we told?" Most of them have been told often enough, but wouldn't listen.)

So I said, "My dear fellow, you must really go and pitch into some-one else about that. I am doing my best. Besides, what did you do about it when you were on Earth; what would you have said supposing I had told you about it?"

And he laughed, and said, "You've got me there Sir. I should have said 'Bunkum'."

Then he said "You know, we over here have no sort of reluctance to talk about God. We live and move and have our being in His light. Why do you people consider it to be so shame-making?"

I hadn't time to answer him then because the power ran low and he was cut off. (He came back the next week to thank us. A very charm-ing person.)

But it is a very pertinent question and it deserves a considered answer.

I think that there are two main reasons. The first is that the intelli-gence of the average twentieth-century man is subconsciously insulted by the fourth-century rigmarole which the shepherds of the Church deal out to their flocks as being a statement of the Eternal Verities. He imagines that confession of belief in God and Christ will be taken as acceptance of the teaching of the Church which is repellent to his instinctive judgment. He is not in fact a disbeliever. Pain and mortal danger will bring the Names of God and of Christ to his lips in heart-felt prayer, he will attend Services of Intercession or Thanksgiving, but to be surprised in the act of personal devotion is shame intolerable.

The second reason is a perfectly healthy revulsion from the idea of being considered a hypocrite by others, or, still more important, by himself. Here it is not Church dogma that he is up against, but Christian ethics. He sees the struggle for existence, and the amassing of first a competence and then a superfluity for himself and his family becomes his primary aim. Then there are certain satisfactions and gratifications whose claims have to be met; and only when this has been done is he prepared to notice and consider the claims of others. Not that he thinks all this out logically in his mind as a rule. He is fundamentally honest; these feelings are instinctive, and he would consider himself a prig and a hypocrite if he went around preaching what he was not prepared to practise.

This attitude, if he was forced to define it, he would describe as one of Enlightened Self-interest, and it would be difficult indeed to gainsay him if his own conception of the Self were to be accepted.

But the object of this chapter, and in fact of this book, is to promote the theory that the true Self is something quite different from the temporary and transient Personality, and that our friend's whole philosophy of the object and conduct of Earth life is based on a fundamental misconception.

If, therefore, I maintain that Enlightened Self-interest consists in leading a completely ethical life, do not regard my attainment as a measure of my sincerity. Do not think me a hypocrite because I fail in the attempt to practise what I preach.

Let me speak in all honesty and simplicity from the heart, believing that what I say is based on common sense and ascertainable fact. Because I want to try to convey to you the atmosphere in which we work. It is difficult enough in any case to convey thoughts by words, and quite impossible if I have to maintain a pose of superior detachment.

What I want to say is that we are members of a great Group, working on both sides of the Valley of the Shadow, and that all our work, every communication, and every action resulting therefrom is directed towards the giving of help or strength or comfort to others.

I was reading an article the other day which spoke in patronising terms of 'The Guides;' It said that some circles regarded their Guides with esteem and affection, and placed great reliance on their words.

And why not, I should like to know? These are no strangers to us. These are our old familiar friends with whom we have lived and loved and fought adown the centuries. Many and varied have been our earthly relationships in the kaleidoscope of time, but through it all has run an indissoluble bond! Who indeed have earned our love and trust if not they?

I shall quote freely in this chapter from what they have given us in the course of our work, both for the intrinsic value of the teaching and also because no words of my own can so well convey the deep intensity of their love for mankind and their passionate desire to tip the balance towards the Light in the dark days which are about us and which lie ahead.

"The task is so tremendous, humanity's need so great, that we must needs work everyone to the uttermost.

"If you could see how terrible is the need. If you could realise as we do how near, how terribly near, to the brink of complete and utter disaster the earth plane is, you would gain some measure of understanding.

"We desire at this time to gather together so much power from you earth-dwellers that when He comes He shall be uplifted, and His power shall flood and shall break asunder all barriers, that hate and sorrow and distress shall be vanquished if only for a single instant, that His power shall linger, and in the great struggle which lies ahead we shall have many reservoirs from which to draw. That every one of His children, even to the last in the outer darkness, shall be seen and reached. It is a mighty task, is it not, and worthy of our greatest efforts?

"I have been serious, my brother, because this work is my life's blood. But you understand. And now I would say a word concerning these assemblies which you visit, and from which we draw so much power.

"I cannot show you their importance in our scheme more clearly than by saying 'Without fuel to feed the engine the aircraft could not rise towards the Star.' The simile was supplied by one of your boys. We have the aircraft, we have the engine, and you people who have the will and the love and the thought supply our fuel.

Therefore I thank you and everyone associated with you in gathering together the people. I thank you as your brother, I thank you as the mouthpiece of these your many friends gathered here at this moment, and I thank you as the ambassador of the King of Kings."

I am told that I have been taken to task by one of the psychic journals for the way in which I have spoken at certain meetings of the Saints and Angels of God. And so I think that a few words on the subject will not be amiss.

On many occasions I have spoken of St. George and King Arthur as living shining active beings, operators at the present moment of two important Rays, and distinguished in particular for their association with England and for the support which they give to the great work which she is being called upon to do in the world.

Now don't suppose for a moment that I attach importance to the question as to whether the Pope of Rome did or did not distinguish any individual by the rite of canonisation. I don't want to offend my Catholic friends, so I will say no more on that subject except to marvel how any human being could assume such a responsibility. The spirits whom we know as St. George and King Arthur are important to us particularly in regard to their functions and associations. Their titles are but names; George is as much a King as Arthur, and Arthur as much a Saint as George. They do not belong to a race apart from humanity, they are human beings, far in advance of us on the path it is true, but of like nature with ourselves. One day, remote as that day may be, every one of us will attain and eventually surpass their present state of development, by which time they will themselves have made a corresponding advance.

One of the important teachings of the Protestant Religion is that worship and adoration should not be paid to the Saints, but reserved for God. This is very right and proper, but it has resulted in a tendency to regard communion with the Saints as a form of idolatry. This is quite erroneous, and, if we adopt this attitude, we deliberately discard a potential source of strength and support.

"He shall give His Angels charge over thee to keep thee in all thy ways." So why should we not take advantage of the love and help and companionship which is ours for the asking?

I don't think I can illustrate the teaching which our circle has received on this subject better than by recounting the circumstances of a service in Westminster Abbey on 23rd April 1944. The occasion was the re-dedication of the Warrior Chapel to St. George, and the date was, of course, St. George's Day.

The service was both beautiful and impressive, but there was a good deal of ceremonial, with rich vestments, banners and processions. Two days later we received the following from Z: —

> "I was at the Ceremonial. It reminded me very much of the days when we took the unenlightened of our people, and, by giving them a picture, tried to bring through one of the eternal truths. Alas that it

is still necessary! There was much power which could be used by that Spirit upon whom so many called. There was only one thought which came to me as I watched. How sad that so many should mistake Him to whom they should call.

"That great and shining Spirit, who so valiantly responds, desires no adoration—but love and comradeship. He is one of us.

"That great uplift of the heart, that Adoration, belongs to One alone. Let not men rise up others in His place. It shackles him whom it should set free. Brother, comrade, friend; hand in hand we walk and he with us raises his head and bends the knee in adoration and love. Under the Mighty One we serve." And so you see that there is some danger of the return swing of the Reformation pendulum carrying us too far in the other direction. Prayer to the Saints, by all means, worship, no.

And now, lest I be misunderstood, I had better say what I conceive to be the essential nature of Prayer, for it is very generally misunderstood. Many people think of Prayer in its lower form as a request to God that He will grant us some personal gift or satisfaction, and in its higher form that God will grant a similar boon to somebody else or perhaps remedy some defect which we observe in the world about us. (I speak of God as if He were an intelligent individual like ourselves, but infinitely wise and powerful. Let it pass for the time being. I will revert to the subject later.) If no appreciable result follows from these exercises, then men say that God does not hear our prayers.

This seems to me to be a very childish conclusion. It infers that God does not know what is going on in His world until we have drawn His attention to some requirement or defect, and that when this has been done He should at once loose His power in the direction indicated by us. It is as though God were some piece of heavy artillery which we could discharge at our pleasure by pressing a trigger.

Then there is another form of prayer which consists in repeating a certain form of words which are meaningless, either because they are spoken in an unknown language or because the thoughts of those praying have, through indefinite repetition, ceased to be associated with the words. Such prayers are little better than incantations. If you happen to belong to the Church of England, you will find it a salutary exercise to make up your mind that you will follow with concentrated attention every word throughout a service—prayers, psalms, hymns, sermon and all—and count up the number of times you catch yourself wool-gathering in some path into which you have been led by an undisciplined mind.

Now I will say without hesitation that God hears every prayer of whatever sort, but different types of prayer have varying effects. The sleepy drone." And finally oh Lord hasten the time when wars shall cease in all the world," and the selfish prayer, "Oh Lord grant that I may win the Calcutta Sweep" are dissipated into the ether almost as soon as uttered.

God has made the laws of Nature, and God operates through natural law, ignorant though we may be of His processes. He also operates like a Commander in Chief through an organised chain of command. He works through His Hierarchy, through the Saints and Angels of whom we have been speaking, through lesser spiritual entities, and finally through US. At each stage a quantum of spiritual power is contributed at the appropriate wave-length, and the point to which I have been leading up is that WE have to make a contribution to the total power which is employed, a contribution which is essential if the work to be done lies on or near the Earth level.

To quote Z again: —

"It was indeed a strong shaft of love and light that you started speeding towards us. Many of those dear ones whom you call boys were awakened and helped while you were speaking. These gatherings do give us a great uplift. If only people would realise how mighty is the power of thought! "Yet perhaps it is well that at the present state of humanity's evolution this power is not understood, you have so misused the powers you have already uncovered. But we do thank you who direct this power in the channel of light, for it is indeed a strong weapon to our hand at a time when strong weapons are needed." Prayer is only thought aimed in the direction of God. But Thought is not necessarily aimed in that direction, unfortunately for humanity.

For thought is real, thought is dynamic, thought does things, and thought moves mountains. When Hitler pours forth his flood of dark mistaken thoughts he and his audience constitute a vast dynamo of lurid power. Do you think you are going to stem that flood by saying "Our Father, gabble, gabble, gabble?"

No. Prayer, which is worth calling Prayer, must come from the mind and the heart, it must build strong and persisting thought-forms, and it must take with it something of the basic essence of ourselves. We should sweat when we really pray. We have a Precedent— at Gethsemane.

Now if we look on prayer in this way, I think we shall find that the fundamentally selfish prayers will not rise in our hearts at all, they Will be too petty and trivial to put in an appearance. Even our prayers for our loved ones will begin to take the form: "God guard him from all evil" rather than, "God bring him back safe to me," and our 'selfish' prayers will take the" form of asking for help in our own efforts to acquire those qualities which will make us more efficient servants to Him and to humanity.

This faculty of building thought-forms, strong and enduring and beneficent, is rather an important one to acquire. After death, spirits soon lose the habit of thinking in words and begin to think in pictures, and if we can visualise our thoughts it not only facilitates and strengthens communication but it automatically eliminates the 'gabble, gabble, gabble 'type of prayer.

You can speak words without thinking of what you are saying, but you can't build a picture without thinking what you are doing.

Try it and see.

It comes to me that the story of the Tower of Babel has significance deeper than its literal interpretation. The first Races of humanity on earth were much less material (literally and metaphorically) than we, and I think that this story symbolises the change in the structure of the human brain which resulted in men beginning to communicate with one another by speech instead of by thought, and consequently to misunderstand one another.

"Stress the power of collective cooperative thought," says Z. "Stress that all are units in a stupendous whole, units held together by the love of the Nameless One. Every unit is important. No matter how humble, no matter how seemingly great, each can contribute something, which no other can give. All bring to Him their failures and their triumphs. Both He accepts with love. His mighty goodness is beyond the tongue of man or of angels to tell.

"What we strive to do is to make it felt among men that they shall turn towards Him, that He may smile upon them.

"My brother, I walk with you among His people and it rejoices me when I hear them hearken to your words; when I see the responsive spark go forth and I know that His plan is being fulfilled. We are but imperfect instruments, but He knows even better than we our frailties. His love forgives everything. There are none so lost that He cannot find them. None so forgotten that He does not remember them. None so lonely that He does not hold them close to His heart.

"It is this message of His great love which Man so sorely needs; for in a full realisation of such love Man himself must come to love all creatures. Only in love and understanding can His plan be completed.

"And now may He incline His ear towards our petitions, may He cleanse our hearts that our lights shall burn clear, may He strengthen our sinews that we falter not in obeying His command.

May that command ring clarion-clear that we shall joyfully spring to its fulfilment, and in His blessing may we rest."

I have been speaking about God in a rather childish way, and I shall continue to do so as a matter of convenience. But a page or two back I promised to revert to the subject. I am taught that everyone and everything is a part of God. The essential you, and the essential I, are parts of God, and therefore we are parts of one another, and therefore we must love one another because a man cannot hate himself. St. George and the depraved sot, the octopus and the butterfly, the mountain and the ocean are all parts of God, and so is the littlest speck of dust on the outermost planet of the farthest galaxy. This I believe to be true, but my human brain cannot reconcile this with the idea of God as an omniscient and infinitely compassionate Being. This is because I have not arrived at, and may not reach for millennia, the stage of at-onement with God, which is the goal of all humanity and all creation.

It might be supposed that this conception of God as a combination of so many and diverse elements might lead the Shining Ones who have reached At onement to regard God as a sort of natural phenomenon to be dispassionately and impersonally regarded; but this is far from being the case.

The higher we reach in our discarnate contacts, the deeper we find the awe and reverence with which that Name is regarded.

"The devils also believe and tremble," and it is left to ignorant self-sufficient Man to take that Name lightly upon his lips. May I quote again Zabdiel from *Many Mansions*. "There is much power in the use of a name. Know this and remember it, for much disaster continually ensues by reason of the misuse of holy names, disaster wondered at and often felt to be unmerited."

There are many mysteries upon which speculation and thought are fruitful, but I believe that the nature of God is not one of these at man's present stage of development. I believe that its very conception is far outside the reach of the human brain. Jesus said "No man cometh to the Father but by me." I do not speculate upon the nature of the Father—whether He is the same as the Absolute, the Nameless One, the Ultimate. I know only that Jesus lived upon Earth and was there overshadowed by the Christ Spirit; and therefore that the combination Jesus-Christ can be visualised by us in our prayers, and furthermore that He is the highest Entity which we are capable of visualising. He is our Mediator, and if therefore we address our prayers to the Father through Him in love and faith, we need not torture our brains with speculations to which we shall find no answer. If we cannot rest without the Answer, we must walk with redoubled humility and zeal along the Path which leads to at-onement.

Of adoration and of thanksgiving I have little to say. God is infinite in compassion and wisdom and He has no need for our worship and gratitude, it is we who have the need to give—to pay our humble tribute in these respects. Truly we must become as little children—not childish but childlike. We must cast back our minds as far as they will take us, to the days when we were little children at our mother's knee; before the cares and responsibilities of the world had moulded our minds into the grooves of materialism and self-sufficiency, and try to recapture the atmosphere of love and trust and innocence in which we then existed. We must return in humility to the starting point before we can go forward. The greatest things in life are the simplest, and the highest Spirits are the most humble.

"As always," says Z, "my message is a message demanding service. Only in serving one another, in drawing closer together in the fellowship of love can mankind even begin to understand the great destiny the Creator has laid out for him.

"Only by bringing to fruition the seed of kindliness which lies deep in every heart, only by bringing to the flowering the love which is our birthright, can we so-called angels and men tread the pathway which will lead eventually to that point of complete understanding, of utter fusion, of At-onement, which is our goal.

"With this ever before us we can but strive to walk humbly that we may go forward unerringly. 'What,' you may ask, 'can we do?' The importance of the part to be played in the Great Song of Creation by the peoples of the earth is not to be overlooked, for theirs is the task of refining the heaviest of matter until it becomes at one with that Spirit within which is life itself.

"Then will frustration, then will twisted thinking, then will hopelessness, fade away, and fulfilment and joy and a pride in being shall be the lot of all mankind. This can be done now. No living soul is so undeveloped, no soul encased in matter so unawakened, no soul so far from Him, that it cannot accept now the staff of life.

"*How* to accept? It is simple, and has been given to men over and over again. Love ye one another.

"The simple kindly thoughts—Hold them, multiply them. The kindly deed—Do it now. The smile, the word of cheer—Now is the time for them.

"Open your hearts. Ask that He will give you understanding. Invite Him to dwell within.

"My words are poor, my brother, to express the glory of the task to which we have been called; but if when you speak to the people you can give them hope, not only in survival beyond physical death but hope in life, hope in the future of the earth, you will have done a great work. For hopelessness and fear are the two shackles we see imprisoning men today.

"Tell them that no matter how great the chaos, how deep the pit, how black the waves with which man surrounds himself—the great power of the Spirit and the deep Love of the Gentle Master can sweep it all away as each individual soul awakens to a realisation of its true destiny, as awaken it must eventually. Of what avail that we should return to you from our place where all is harmony, if we cannot bring to you even a little of that harmony—if we cannot show you that His Love is boundless, and that against it everything battles in vain.

"Tell the people, my brother, that out of this time of trial and testing they can rise to nobler heights, if each one will take to himself and live a full life, accepting all experience, and keeping before him a living injunction, 'Do ye unto your brother as ye would he should do unto you.'

"There you have the secret of life. Let men clothe it in what words they will. When you can identify yourself with the joy and with the sorrow of your brother—then have you tasted the living waters and never shall you thirst or hunger again.

"It is old. It has been since the beginning, that which I have told you. How much longer will it be before men realise the simplicity of it. Oh, how you complicate your lives."

Now I want to give you a short message from Z on the responsibility of this country for using her great influence on the side of the Light at the Peace Table and in the difficult years which will come after the war: —

"Very soon now this little island will be put to the test. It is no exaggeration when I tell you that the future of mankind rests with the outpouring from this Country. It can be completely destructive, so great is the power invested here, or it can be turned from destruction to construction and the harvest of the sword may be reaped in glory.

"You must give to us every atom of power that we may weld the hearts of men, who go forth, in one purpose; that all who would withstand and destroy the flame of the living spirit shall once more be vanquished, and all men be raised out of the sacrifice and the tears, one step nearer Home, one step nearer to Him. It can be done and it shall be done. The great Wave of Love shall go forth with them, that the darkness shall recede before the Light of Him who so loves mankind.'

We are the centre and heart of the Empire. The Empire, with the rest of the English-speaking world, have a preponderating voice in the councils of the Allies, and it is the Allies who must plot the new course for the labouring ship of the world when this great tempest dies away. And so what we here in Britain think and say and do is of vital importance to the future of the Earth.

I have spoken of the overwhelming power of Thought and Prayer, and I have shown that Prayer is potent in proportion to its intensity, but if millions of people pray the effect is obviously very greatly increased, while, if they all pray simultaneously the effect will be overwhelming.

I want, therefore, to draw the attention of those who do not already participate in it to the Big Ben Silent Minute observance, in conjunction with the striking of Big Ben at 9 p.m. on the Home Service radio programme. Keep this Silent Minute in your homes and ask your friends to do the same. Think first of your dear ones in peril and of those who have already made the great sacrifice, and then reach up to the Source of all Power and Light and Love and send out from your heart the strongest wave of light which you can generate. Think of it as chasing the darkness out of every corner of this Country, and then spreading across the sea to the tortured continents so that the whole World may be bathed in a glow of golden radiance, hold the thought of Brotherhood. This is indeed a blessed work and we have been told from more than one source of the effect that has already been produced. If this little book can serve still further to intensify that effect, it will not have been written in vain.

And now I draw towards the end of my task. I acknowledge with humility the inadequacy of the last chapter of *Many Mansions*. How sterile was that argument on the subject of Atonement! We should not spend our energies in thinking about our personal salvation. How can any soul be 'saved' while others are in torment and while the Earth is filled with lust and fear and hatred?

Both here and hereafter must we devote ourselves to the service of humanity in selfless sacrifice.

As Z says in one of his blessings: —

"And now we raise unto Him the offering of ourselves, all that we are, in His service. May His blessing pour upon us and in His love may we go forth to labour in His Vineyard, counting neither the *cost* nor the *reward*. For His power envelops us, and His strength is our staff. Amen."

This is the true Spiritualism, the Giving rather than the Receiving, the glad and happy comradeship with the Saints and Angels of God for the service of mankind in The Beloved Master's Name. It is an aspect unknown and undiscovered by the critics of Spiritualism, and but dimly realised even by some of its adherents. It is not a Religion, it is Religion.

And Z has a message for mediums too. He writes: —

"Behind all this is a great movement of the Spirit. The Spirit shall triumph. But, that it may be a mighty triumph, let those who have been given the inestimable privilege of guarding the Light of the Spirit, see to it by their thoughts even more than by their conduct that no wind shall blow it out.

"For only the guardians of the flame can quench its brightness by allowing themselves to be unworthy. All others blow against it in vain."

I fear that I have rather given the impression that Z is the only spokesman of our Group. In this I have done an injustice to others, and particularly to Chang, who specialises in the healing work.

I must give you a sample of his beautiful Oriental style. On this occasion he was introducing a visitor who had come to us for the first time to give us special help at a difficult stage.

"May the fragrance of a hundred blossoms caress your nostrils and the wisdom of ten thousand sages chime in your hearts. I bring to you greetings from one of our Elder Brethren. He wishes to speak to you if we can arrange the channel. Hearken well to his words, for his tongue has the wisdom of the serpent and the beauty of bells at evening when the temple is still."

Then the 'Light bearer' spoke, but his message was for us alone. Afterwards Chang continued: —

"He has placed his sandals upon your feet that ten thousand horses may not pull them from the pathway, and the fragrance which rises from the garden under the moon he twines around your hearts that you may remember what he has told you.

"Greetings to you from our brothers, and may the blessing which sweeps through the forest in the song of a bird, the blessing which descends in the sunlight and the rain, rest upon you."

Is it surprising that we should love them?

And now I want to link up everything I have written in this book into one final conclusion, the importance of which cannot be exaggerated. This conclusion is that the time has now arrived when the wisdom of the Ancient Mysteries is to be added to and enriched by the message of Jesus the Christ.

The combination will form the basis of a World Religion, which will satisfy the aspirations of the mystic and the intelligence of the scientist.

This conviction has been increasingly borne in upon me for some time past, and so you may imagine the interest with which I received the following message from Mrs. Hill. As you will see, part of it was written on the top of Glastonbury Tor, and part in the Abbey grounds. 'C.M.H.' is Mrs. Hill, 'Father' is Colonel Gascoigne, and Olga is a friend who was on earth until about eighteen months ago.

Written on the top of Glastonbury Tor, August 5th 1944.

C.M.H. "Shall we write?" Father. "Yes, but briefly, this is a tremendously strong centre, and I may not be able to hold the link. Here is Olga; she says she understands this place."

Olga. "Oh, Cynthia, do you know where you are? This place is the centre of all the old Atlantean teaching, and I am being shown, through you, the great influences that brought it into being. These wonderful beings who outstripped all other races in the quest of knowledge, and incidentally overlooked the need for spiritual advancement in themselves ... I see many of these great beings around you here. Mountain spirits, creatures of marvellous beauty, they are quite unearthly and belong to another range of existence altogether.

"Now I'm going to ask you to go back into the Abbey grounds and write with me there. This is too strong; I cannot direct the power."

In the Abbey grounds.

"Now I can write much more easily. Here is a kindly softened power - it is entirely different. Now I must go slowly and explain.

"I see this place as a network of forces, all having different colours, mingling and intermingling like a cascade of water in the sunshine, but the colours do not merge, they remain unchanged, they weave their way in and out, some in unison, some in opposition to the rest, but mainly in conjunction with them in order to perfect the whole.

"The atmosphere on the Tor was Primeval, here it is Christian, and Mediaeval. The two powers form a contrast to each other, and we can, if we keep our minds open and unbiased, form the link between these two forces.

"You and I have often lost interest in the Christian Church because of its simplicity and lack of technique as shown by the other great

Eastern religions. They carried with them an immense load of philosophy, and like a luggage train they had to move slowly. Into this slow moving world came Jesus, the Christ. He came as an athlete, stripped of all but the essentials. Christ did not come in order to bring us another step further but to leap forward into the unknown regions of the LOVE planes. It was as though the Great Spirit was impatient, and a bridgehead had to be won across the river of ignorance. Christ, came as a commando equipped with the one thing which He came to impress upon the ether, LOVE . . . and His followers have for many centuries tried to emulate His simplicity, and the Church had at first to remain aloof from all other creeds while they were still struggling as it were on the slippery slopes of disbelief; these athletes, who followed their great Leader, had to be blind to all but the goal that lay ahead.

"Since then we have gathered knowledge and time has enabled the slow-moving philosophies to catch up with the advanced guard, and it has been prepared that at certain places the two worlds of thought and feeling can meet. This and Iona are two of the meeting places where the ancient wisdom and the Christ Love unite. Not the teaching of the Church, but after centuries of pain, suffering and disappointment, the essence of the original teaching has emerged; and here we have the Christ Ray enfolding the Abbey and all the ruined buildings.

"The important point is that NOW, at this moment, the complete union of these two worlds is vital. It was effected once in the person of King Arthur and his Knights. By the way, that is all as true as anything in the world. But they killed the King, and his followers were scattered, and the material thought of the new age flowed over his memory.

"Now Germany has allied herself openly with the ancient wisdom. She willingly threw herself open to the old influences, and they have used her until she became possessed. Of course the Great Ones have not allowed this to be wasted; they have put it all to some good use. But Germany has to relearn and redirect her mind and withdraw from this terrible vibration of cruelty where the Christ love is shunned and all is dark and hopeless. The cult of Arthur and his Knights must return to save the world and bring happiness back to life. I am so weary, Darling; I can't tell you what hard work it is trying to make you think my thoughts, but I'll get them through somehow."

Note the reference to Iona. As I said in my remarks on the Rays, there are power-centres in many parts of this country and elsewhere. These power-centres have in some way to be linked up and the power released into a sort of grid-system, similar to that organised to convey electricity from the great powerhouses to the points of consumption. I wish I knew more about this, because I am sure that it is very important.

But this I know, that enlightenment will come to those who are to be used for the work, and the great Plan will go forward—forward inexorably towards the goal, which is the flooding of the World with Light and the elimination of the darkness from every nook and cranny—for that is what we mean when we pray with every atom of energy we possess " Thy Kingdom Come."

And now let Z finish this book for me with one of his lovely prayers, and may the Blessing of the Most High be upon it and upon all you who read it.

"Let us raise our hearts and ask His Blessing, for without His Power we can accomplish nothing.

"Thou Nameless One, whose children we are, turn Thy Countenance towards us, and raise us up, so that we may see Thy Smile; that we may be cleansed and refreshed, and that we may be worthy channels through which Thy Power may flow to a sorely distressed humanity.

"We seek to serve Thee. Grant unto us Thy Strength that we may say in truth ' Thy Will be done.'"

Grant unto us Thy Love, that we may be worthy servants, that our mistakes may be made in Love and so be acceptable unto Thee. And unto Thee we offer ourselves; for Thine is all Praise and all Glory throughout the timeless ages. Amen."

Paperbacks also available from
White Crow Books

Jesus of Nazareth with Simon Parke—
Conversations with Jesus of Nazareth
ISBN 978-1-907661-41-9

Thomas à Kempis with Simon
Parke—*The Imitation of Christ*
ISBN 978-1-907661-58-7

Julian of Norwich with Simon
Parke—*Revelations of Divine Love*
ISBN 978-1-907661-88-4

Allan Kardec—*The Spirits Book*
ISBN 978-1-907355-98-1

Allan Kardec—*The Book on Mediums*
ISBN 978-1-907661-75-4

Emanuel Swedenborg—*Heaven and Hell*
ISBN 978-1-907661-55-6

P.D. Ouspensky—*Tertium Organum:
The Third Canon of Thought*
ISBN 978-1-907661-47-1

Dwight Goddard—*A Buddhist Bible*
ISBN 978-1-907661-44-0

Michael Tymn—*The Afterlife Revealed*
ISBN 978-1-970661-90-7

Michael Tymn—*Transcending the
Titanic: Beyond Death's Door*
ISBN 978-1-908733-02-3

Guy L. Playfair—*If This Be Magic*
ISBN 978-1-907661-84-6

Guy L. Playfair—*The Flying Cow*
ISBN 978-1-907661-94-5

Guy L. Playfair —*This House is Haunted*
ISBN 978-1-907661-78-5

Carl Wickland, M.D.—
Thirty Years Among the Dead
ISBN 978-1-907661-72-3

John E. Mack—*Passport to the Cosmos*
ISBN 978-1-907661-81-5

Peter & Elizabeth Fenwick—
The Truth in the Light
ISBN 978-1-908733-08-5

Erlendur Haraldsson—
Modern Miracles
ISBN 978-1-908733-25-2

Erlendur Haraldsson—
At the Hour of Death
ISBN 978-1-908733-27-6

Erlendur Haraldsson—
The Departed Among the Living
ISBN 978-1-908733-29-0

Brian Inglis—*Science and Parascience*
ISBN 978-1-908733-18-4

Brian Inglis—*Natural and Supernatural:
A History of the Paranormal*
ISBN 978-1-908733-20-7

Ernest Holmes—*The Science of Mind*
ISBN 978-1-908733-10-8

Victor & Wendy Zammit —*A Lawyer
Presents the Evidence For the Afterlife*
ISBN 978-1-908733-22-1

Casper S. Yost—*Patience
Worth: A Psychic Mystery*
ISBN 978-1-908733-06-1

William Usborne Moore—
Glimpses of the Next State
ISBN 978-1-907661-01-3

William Usborne Moore—
The Voices
ISBN 978-1-908733-04-7

John W. White—
The Highest State of Consciousness
ISBN 978-1-908733-31-3

Stafford Betty—
The Imprisoned Splendor
ISBN 978-1-907661-98-3

Paul Pearsall, Ph.D. —
Super Joy
ISBN 978-1-908733-16-0

All titles available as eBooks, and selected titles available in Hardback and Audiobook formats from www.whitecrowbooks.com

Lightning Source UK Ltd.
Milton Keynes UK
UKHW011250100221
378556UK00003B/897